FX Law and Regulations in Korea

International Banking and Securities Law

Volume published in this Brill Research Perspectives title are listed at *brill.com/rpbs*

FX Law and Regulations in Korea

Problems and Prospects

By

Min-woo Kang

BRILL

LEIDEN | BOSTON

This paperback book edition is simultaneously published as issue 4.2–3 of *International Banking and Securities Law* DOI: 10.1163/24056936-12340011.

Library of Congress Control Number: 2022950478

Brill Open Access options can be found at brill.com/openaccess.

Typeface for the Latin, Greek, and Cyrillic scripts: "Brill". See and download: brill.com/brill-typeface.

ISBN 978-90-04-54029-3 (paperback)
ISBN 978-90-04-54057-6 (e-book)

This book is printed on acid-free paper and produced in a sustainable manner.

Contents

FX Law and Regulations in Korea: Problems and Prospects

Min-woo Kang | ORCID: 0000-0001-9933-7508
Lecturer in Banking and Finance, Korea University of School of Law [02841]
145 Anam-ro, Seongbuk-gu, Seoul, Korea
minwoo_kang@korea.ac.kr

Abstract

The last two decades of the Korean foreign exchange market regulations, especially aftermath the 1997 Asian financial crisis, can be characterised by an increased emphasis on the capital account liberalisation and deregulation. Although several new types of regulatory measures were implemented to enhance market resilience in the midst of the 2008 global financial crisis, strict control measures were largely eased in order to facilitate cross border trades. However, there are still many remaining unresolved problems and the rapidly changing financial environment poses new challenges for legal institutions surrounding the foreign exchange market. This contribution aims to shed some light on the Korean government's efforts to facilitate foreign transactions, while maintaining equilibrium in the balance of payments and stabilising the value of currency by regulating the external shock-sensitive market. It also offers some insight for the authorities to consider to improve the legal system by providing an in-depth analysis of the recent notable changes in the regulatory landscape.

Keywords

Foreign Exchange Transactions Act – foreign exchange bank system – capital control – macroprudential regulation – currency rigging – anti-money laundering legislation

 | DOI:10.1163/9789004540576_002

1 Introduction

Korea is a small open economy whose domestic policies do not, if ever, affect world prices (such as interest rates, exchange rates) but take them as given.[1] On a related note, the Korean economy has shown to be vulnerable to external disturbances. Indeed, Korea has to date experienced the devastating currency crisis twice: one is the 1997 Asian financial crisis and the other is the 2008 global financial crisis.[2]

Such vulnerability is mainly due to the fact that Korea is not an issuing country whose currency (the Korean Won, KRW) is not a key currency that is generally used for international trade and investment. Outside of the fundamental problem of what is called *original sin* that most emerging market economies commonly suffer from, however, there is one more critical issue that has drawn the Korean policy markers' attention. A relatively low liquidity and lack of sufficient market depth often triggered extreme volatility of the foreign exchange (FX) market (i.e., large swings of exchange rates) when it is faced with economic shocks, which was partly because the Korean financial markets excessively relied on external short-term funds (or short-term borrowing), not long-term finance.

In this respect, it becomes clear that the overarching policy goal that the Korean FX law (the Foreign Exchange Transactions Act, or the FETA) that governs the foreign exchange markets and exchange rate system in Korea should focus on facilitating foreign exchange transactions and promoting the development of capital markets that raise funds at the longer end of the maturity spectrum, while ensuring stability in the FX market. If so, has the FETA and its regulatory system made it to this policy goal? To be sure, much progress has been made since its inception in 1998 (when it repealed and replaced the former *Foreign Exchange Control Act*) but unfortunately, there are still many remaining problems. It is widely accepted that enormously complex procedure regulations, including pre-trades reporting obligations of transactional details, are burdensome, being an obstacle to free FX transactions. Furthermore, the long-standing "foreign exchange bank system", which indicates that authorised banks can operate any FX business, but other industry players, such as securities firms or insurance companies, may participate in the market to a

1 One of the defining features of small open economies is that a financial instrument traded in international markets are not priced by domestic factors but its prices are largely determined in international markets. See Quintana (2013), p 9.

2 Currency crisis can be defined as "in addition to a nominal depreciation of 25 percent, at least a doubling in the rate of depreciation with respect to the previous year and a rate of depreciation the previous year below 40 percent". See Milesi-Ferretti and Razin (1998), p 22.

very limited extent, has been under criticism for the reason that it keeps the market from being a level playing field. Although the government's regulatory stance has recently changed considerably enough, the way the authority takes to reform was not systematic just like a band-aid method; that is, amending administrative rules on an ad hoc basis, which has made the complex legal system even more complicated and confusing.

This contribution re-examines the Korean FX law and regulations to tackle the inherent problems in the regulatory system, especially taking the policy rationale behind it seriously. Particularly, in an attempt to overhaul the legal system in a systematic manner, we also call for amending the rules of other financial laws, such as the Financial Investment Services and Capital Markets Act (FISCMA) and anti-money laundering legislations. This is because foreign exchange transactions cannot be properly regulated by a single law but rather the policy objectives can be fully achieved only if other financial laws work congruent with foreign exchange law and regulations.

2 Theoretical Underpinnings of FX Regulations

2.1 *Legal and Economic Aspect of Currency Assets*

FX products traded in the markets are either foreign currencies or any derivatives contracts whose underlying assets are foreign currencies. Therefore, analysing the characteristics of currency assets would be a good starting point to legally define FX products and to derive their regulatory implications. To begin with, a foreign currency has *moneyness* in that it can be used for international payments for cross-border trade and investment.[3] However, it is worth noting that the usefulness of a foreign currency as a payment measure can be limited unless it is a major key (or anchor) currency that is widely recognised as a reliable money and thus is globally used for international trade and commerce. This is because a foreign currency is not generally a legal tender in countries other than the issuing country.

More pertinent to this discussion is the fact that almost every country has its national currency issued on the basis of the doctrine of monetary sovereignty.

3 Money is generally defined as anything that functions as i) a universal medium of exchange, ii) a measure of value or a standard of contractual obligations, iii) a store of value or wealth, iv) a unit of account, and the most definitive feature of it is that money is a commodity accepted by general consent as a medium of economic exchange. see Proctor (2005), pp 9–10. As money is interchangeable with any goods or services in the economy and used to settle a debt or meet any contractual obligation and, in particular, the government legally forces the acceptance, it is also called *legal tender*.

Each country has its own right to issue the money and regulate the monetary system, which is commonly accepted as a general principle under the international law.[4] In terms of monetary law, this sovereignty-centred argument is closely related to the *state theory of money* developed by a German scholar, Georg F. Knapp, who set forth *chartalism*, claiming that "money is a creature of law".[5] Of course, there are alternative doctrines, such as the *societary theory of money* that stresses the role of societal acceptance of moneyness rather than sovereignty of a state, or the *institutional theory of money* that places more importance on the central bank's authority to control the quantity of money in circulation, because the credibility of monetary system is ultimately dependent upon the value of the currency (i.e., purchasing power of money). It is perceived that the state theory of money provides a clearer view of the legal aspect of money, notwithstanding, in the sense that a sovereign nation has the sole right to issue its money (by delegating the power to the central bank) and own the ultimate authority to govern its monetary system.[6]

Although a foreign currency can be used for commercial needs, it also has an investment attribute. The value of it, usually expressed as an exchange rate, constantly fluctuates with changes in demand and supply for the currency in the market, exposing market participants to risk of losing their principal as well as earn a profit.[7] Investment attributes for currency trades can be easily verified using the Markowitz's modern portfolio theory (MPT).[8] MPT, or mean-variance analysis demonstrates that "investment risk can be minimised for the same portfolio by holding a combination of instruments (from different asset classes) that are not perfectly positively correlated".[9] Simply put, as shown in the following formula for portfolio return variance (σ_p^2), "less correlated asset pairs reduce portfolio risk proxied by return variance".[10]

4 The Permanent Court of International Justice earlier acknowledged the validity of monetary sovereignty in 1929. See Lastra (2006), pp 16–17.

5 See Proctor, *supra* n. 3, pp 15–16.

6 Lastra, *supra* n. 4, p 21.

7 The rate of return of any financial assets denominated in a foreign currency can be decomposed into the rate of return of the asset at issue (i.e., its local return) and the exchange rates changes. For example, the return on a foreign bond is calculated equal to $c - D \times \Delta FY + s$, where c is current yield, D is bond duration, ΔFY is change in the yield, and s is the percentage change in the exchange rate.

8 Kang (2019), p 235.

9 Ibid., p 236.

10 Ibid. The correlation coefficient (ρ), a statistical measure that calculates the strength of the relationship between variables, ranges from –1 to 1. A negative relationship indicates two relevant variables (here, assets) move in opposite directions, which means the idiosyncratic risk that each asset has can be diversified away in a portfolio.

$$\sigma_p^2 = \sum_i w_i^2 \sigma_i^2 + \sum_i \sum_{j \neq i} w_i w_j \sigma_i \sigma_j \rho_{ij}$$

where w is the fraction(weight) held in an asset, σ is the standard deviation of returns on each asset, and ρ is the correlation coefficient between the returns on assets i and j.

Today, investors know well the benefits of diversification in investing, and thus build portfolios from a collective pool of assets including a foreign currency.[11] Table 1 below shows that the performance of a portfolio that is invested in traditional instruments (stocks or bonds) and alternative investments (commodities or hedge funds) can be improved with the inclusion of a currency asset. Having a negative correlation, a currency asset (here, US dollar) and all other assets "move in the opposite direction", implying that investors can "enhance return with lower risk" through adding a foreign currency to their existing portfolios.[12]

TABLE 1 Matrix of correlation coefficients with asset classes, Jan 1989 to Jun 2016

	S&P 500	Barclays Aggregates	USD	Bloomberg Commodities	HFRI Global Macro
S&P 500	1.00				
Barclays Aggregates	0.12	1.00			
USD	−0.30	−0.22	1.00		
Bloomberg Commodities	0.30	0.04	−0.54	1.00	
HFRI Global Macro	0.32	0.29	−0.11	0.26	1.00

Note: Bloomberg Commodities begins January 1991 and HFRI Global Macro begins January 1990.
SOURCE: RESEARCH AFFILIATES, LLC, USING DATA FROM DATASTREAM, BLOOMBERG, COMMODITIES RESEARCH BOARD, AND GLOBAL FINANCIAL DATA (COPYRIGHT 2016, RESEARCH AFFILIATES. FROM "SYSTEMATIC GLOBAL MACRO", ORIGINALLY PUBLISHED ON WWW.RESEARCHAFFILIATES.COM. REPRODUCED AND REPUBLISHED WITH PERMISSION. ALL RIGHTS RESERVED).

11 A (foreign) currency deems as an asset class, because it has a return-risk profile that is distinctive from other asset classes. For general criteria for determining asset class status, see Kirtzman (1999).

12 Kang, *supra* n. 8, p 236.

The way a foreign currency is treated like an investment vehicle is also found in the accounting practices. International Accounting Standards (IAS) 21 takes into account the fact a purchase and sale of foreign currencies may incur gains or losses from foreign currency translation adjustments, and it thus requires an entity to reflects the effects of changes in foreign exchange rates when reporting financial statements.[13]

Taken together, a foreign currency can be defined as a financial asset that can be used as "a means of international payment" and "a financial instrument".[14] The Korean FETA defines the foreign exchange as "means of international payments, securities, derivatives and claims in foreign currency" and "claims in a foreign currency" means claims denominated in a foreign currency, or those payable in a foreign country.[15] That is, FX products in Korea broadly encompass any financial instruments or claims in a foreign currency, including a foreign currency itself.

2.2 *Unique Features of the FX Market*

The foreign exchange market today operates in a global network, allowing governments, banks, financial institutions, funds, corporations, and individual investors to daily trade massive volumes of currency assets around the globe.[16] Moreover, it is not an organised, over-the-counter (OTC) market in which traders in the largest banks play a dominant role with little, if any, government regulations.

In addition to this, the Korean FX market has the following characteristics. First, the share of spot trades is around 40%, being larger than that of other advanced economies (30% or so), and derivatives trades such as currency swaps or options are not much popular, merely accounting for 2~3%. Second,

---

13 International Accounting Standards 21, available at https://www.ifrs.org/issued-standards/list-of-standards/ias-21-the-effects-of-changes-in-foreign-exchange-rates/.

14 Francis A. Mann, a preeminent legal scholar, once claimed that a foreign currency deemed as "a commodity". According to his *commodity theory of money*, a foreign currency is not "a medium of exchange" used for payment but "a commodity" that is tradable on a specific condition between a buyer and a seller. As such, it is an object that meets debt obligations when it is physically delivered to the counterparty. However, it is generally agreed that such a commodity feature of foreign money has no, if any, significance in modern economies where international payments and settlements via the correspondent banking system are commonplace. Perhaps, foreign money as a commodity would be relevant in very exceptional circumstances where it is traded for a collective purpose (e.g., rare coins or notes). See Proctor, *supra* n. 3, pp 44–46.

15 Art. 3(1) of the FETA.

16 The Bank for International Settlement (BIS) reports that trading in foreign exchange markets averaged $6.6 trillion per day in April 2019. See BIS (2019), p 3.

the trading volume of FX trades is somewhat low relative to the size of the economy, especially in terms of merchandise exports and imports.[17] Third, a heavy reliance on US Dollar (75.1% for spot trades, 80.9% for derivatives trades) and the fact that most interbank transactions are conducted through a small number of brokers (i.e., a broker market), as opposed to advanced economies markets in which FX dealer banks directly trade each other and take a crucial part as market makers (i.e., a dealer market), often makes the Korean FX market vulnerable to even small external disturbances.

2.3 *Policy Rationales for FX Regulation and Supervision*

2.3.1 Protecting against Extreme Exchange Rate Volatility and Securing Financial Stability

If we accept the notion that a foreign currency is an instrument that can be used for both payment and investment, exchange rate, which refers to the domestic currency price of one unit of foreign currency, deems "an asset price".[18] The equilibrium exchange rate is determined in the foreign exchange market by the forces of supply and demand, where demand for foreign currencies arises from the need for importers to pay exporters for importation of goods, or the need for investors to put money into overseas projects, and conversely, supply of foreign currencies occurs when exporters receive payments from importers abroad, or when foreign investors make the purchase of domestic assets.

What a foreign exchange rate is equivalent to an asset price indicates that it continuously changes depending on the market conditions. Exchange rate variation not only adjusts the balance of payments through changes in the relative prices of export and import but also has enormous influence on trading and investment decisions of household, corporations and the government, further effecting on consumer prices, employment, and an overall economy. Therefore, almost all countries today cautiously choose their exchange rate arrangement in accordance with the phase of development of the financial markets and the real economy.

Exchange rate arrangements are generally categorised "on the basis of their degree of flexibility and the existence of formal or informal commitments to exchange rate path" as follows: i) fixed (or pegged) system, ii) floating (or flexible) system, and iii) other managed arrangement, and fixed and floating regimes are in turn divided into their subtypes.[19] To begin with, fixed or pegged regime refers to a system that a country "(formally or de facto) pegs its currency

17 BOK (2022).

18 Krugman et al. (2014), pp 374–378.

19 For a detailed description and explanation of each exchange rate regime, see IMF (2004).

at a fixed rate to another currency or a basket of currencies".[20] In general, a country adopts the fixed rate system when the economy has a high degree of dependence on a particular country, or when the monetary authority lacks policy credibility. By contrast, floating or flexible regime refers to a system that allows exchange rates to vary with the market conditions. It is thus perceived to be well suited for large economies that have a developed and sophisticated financial system. And there are various types of regimes between these two extremes, depending on how much variability a regime allows. Below is the latest survey result that the International Monetary Fund (IMF) conducted,

TABLE 2 Classification of exchange rate arrangements (as of 30 April 2020)

Fixed regime	Hard peg	No separate legal tender	Ecuador, El Salvador, Kosovo, Panama, etc. (13)
		Currency board	Grenada, Hong Kong SAR, Bulgaria, etc. (11)
	Soft peg	Conventional (fixed) peg	Bahrain, Fiji, Iraq, Jordan, Nepal, Oman, Qatar, Saudi Arabia, United Arab Emirates, etc. (41)
		Stabilised arrangement	Bolivia, Iran, Lebanon, Nigeria, Vietnam, etc. (23)
		Crawling peg	Botswana, Honduras, Nicaragua, (3)
		Crawl-like arrangement	Algeria, Bangladesh, Dominican Republic, Ethiopia, Liberia, Rwanda, Singapore, etc. (23)
		Pegged exchange rate within horizontal bands	–
Floating regime		Floating	Belarus, Brazil, Hungary, Iceland, Indonesia, Israel, Korea, Malaysia, Philippines, Thailand, Turkey, etc. (32)
		Free floating	Australia, Canada, France, Germany, Italy, Japan, Mexico, Poland, Russia, Spain, United Kingdom, etc. (31)
Residual		Other managed arrangement	Afghanistan, China, Myanmar, Pakistan, Syria, Venezuela, Zimbabwe, etc. (15)

Note: The number of countries is indicated in parentheses.
SOURCE: IMF (2021)

20 Ibid.

showing that each country across the globe has adopted its own exchange rate arrangement that is most likely to be in its best interest.[21]

Provided that the governmental authority sets monetary stability (or its currency value) as a paramount goal of FX regulation, it seems likely that the fixed regime is superior to the floating one. Literally, the fixed rate system keeps the pegged exchange rate stable, thereby making it possible to remove much of the economic uncertainty stemming from the exchange rate fluctuation. However, we know too well that fixed regime has been so vulnerable to the external shock when the economy was in trouble (e.g., experiencing economic stagnation, a persistent fiscal or current account deficit, or excessive monetary expansion).[22] The fixed rate system has been fragile during speculative attacks, especially when a government forcibly tried to keep its currency value constant by intervening in foreign exchange markets. Given limited foreign reserve assets, central banks could not maintain stability in the value of their currency when there occurred a massive volume of capital outflows, or otherwise, even when market participants merely built up an expectation that there would be large capital outflows.[23] There are indeed numerous examples of such crises. As is well known, Black Wednesday (occurred on 16 September 1992) when a crash of the pound sterling forced the UK government to exit the European Exchange Rate System (ERM) after a failed defence against traders' huge short positions in the currency, has become a classical example. We also find similar patterns of outbreak of crisis in the 1994 tequila (Mexican peso) crisis and in the 1997 Asian financial crisis.

Under floating rate system, on the contrary, a currency value (relative to other currency pair) is allowed to fluctuate in response to changes in the market conditions. At least in theory, exchange rates are expected to move toward market equilibrium in which balance of payments (BOP) must be zero. For example, when a trade deficit happens in a country, excess demand for foreign currencies arises and exchange rate (i.e., the relative price of a foreign currency in terms of a domestic currency) tends to rise, which means that the value of a domestic currency falls (or depreciates). In such a circumstance, export price

21 Since the floating rate system was recognised as a new exchange rate arrangement at the IMF meeting held in Kingston, Jamaica in 1976, each country has selected to operate an appropriate exchange rate system in consideration of the various conditions such as economic size, volume of trade, external debt position, and the financial market development. In particular, the Kingston system went of the gold standard, abolishing the fair price of gold, the function of gold as an international currency. In doing so, it formalised the transition to the variable exchange rate system.

22 For an insightful explanation of the mechanism of currency crisis under the fixed rate regime, see Krugman (1979).

23 Currency crisis of this type is thus called a "self-fulling expectation" crisis in many literatures. See Obstfeld and Rogoff (1996).

competitiveness of the country's products improves, which would in turn contribute to bringing the current account deficit to zero. However, noteworthy here is that floating regime is not a panacea. Uncontrolled cross-border capital flows and overreactions in the foreign exchange market may trigger financial turmoil and greater economic uncertainty. In fact, there is no definite answer to the question of whether there exists a particularly superior regime. Every country should be precautious in assessing the current status of the market development and adopt an adequate exchange rate system.

FX authorities intervene in the currency market when necessary to stabilise the exchange rates and manage the pace of capital flows. To this end, almost all authorities use capital control-like measures, even though there is much difference in the degree of restrictions. Capital controls can be justified in that it is a prerequisite for a sovereign country's independent exercise of monetary policy while stabilising the value of domestic currency. This is what the classical theory of "policy trilemma" (or impossible trinity) claims: out of three policy objectives "free capital mobility", "exchange rate management" and "monetary autonomy", only two are possible and a country has no option but to choose legs of the triangle (A, B, or C) as shown in Figure 1. That is, it is impossible to attain these three goals at the same time. Consider a central bank whose economy is financially liberalised cuts its benchmark interest rate (or inject money into the market) to support economic growth. In such a situation, capital outflow pressure will be heightened, making the value of the domestic currency fall against foreign currencies of countries providing a higher interest rate. If the country operates a fixed rate system, the central bank must sell foreign currencies and buy back domestic currencies enough to restore the existing exchange rate parity. The result is that monetary expansion will be ineffective, and the same logic applies to the case of monetary contraction. Therefore, in order to use the monetary policy tools as a macroeconomic stabiliser, the country must choose between exchange rate variability and capital controls.[24] On a related note, more recent evidence also supports the proposition that capital controls contribute to promoting monetary autonomy and to avoiding sharp exchange rate fluctuations.[25]

---

24 See the Nobel laureate Mundell (1963)'s seminal work. More recently, taking into account the fact that US monetary policy as "a source of credit" plays a dominant role in creating the global financial cycle, some economists argue that a country's monetary policy can be impotent under the condition of free capital mobility, irrespective of whether it allows exchange rate to freely fluctuate or not. According to this reasoning, "independent monetary policies are possible if and only if the capital account is managed". Thus, it is called "policy dilemma or irreconcilable duo". See Rey (2015).

25 Magud et al. (2011).

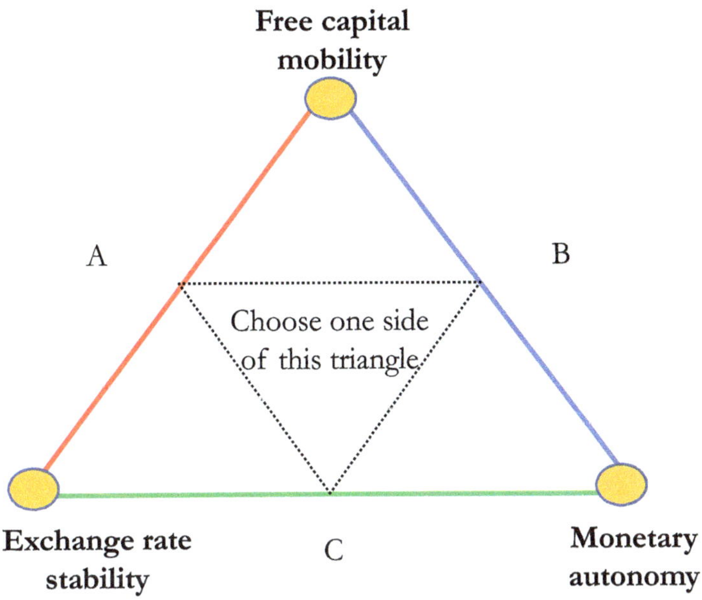

FIGURE 1 Policy trilemma or impossible trinity of open economies

In addition to ordinary central bank market interventions and capital controls, moderating adverse effects of exchange rate volatility on financial markets and real economy is possible through the well-targeted capital flow management policies. Aiming at reducing the costs of credit *boom and bust cycle* that refers to alternating phases of credit growth and decline in the market, the policy measures usually restrict excessive "short-term foreign currency borrowing (or external debt)" and in doing so, they enable an economy to alleviate the shock when a *sudden stop* in the flow of foreign capital into the economy and capital flows reversal abruptly happens. Indeed, this policy option, what is called macroprudential FX regulation, has drawn intense attention from regulators around the world after the 2008 global financial crisis.

The reason why regulating short-term foreign borrowing matters is that it may give rise to a *pecuniary externality* that refers to "an externality that is manifested in a change in prices" in the whole financial markets.[26] It is not a market failure, in that the change in prices is the outcome of optimisation process in a competitive market. However, it creates market inefficiency when the market is incomplete or market participants are subject to financial constraints. Also, it may cause financial amplification. In general, "increases in borrowing and

26 Shubik (1971), p 713.

in collateral prices feed each other during booms, whereas in busts, the feedback turns negative, with credit constraints leading to asset price declines and further tightening of credit".[27] The same logic applies to foreign exchange markets. Foreign exchange liquidity that flows into an economy, which is largely in the form of short-term borrowing in normal times, abruptly dries up in the event of a crisis. It causes exchange rates to spike up and thereby the burden of external debt repayment on domestic entities to surge, accelerating the vicious cycle of fire sales and further declines of the value of the currency.[28] For this reason, many countries have implemented macroprudential FX regulations that target banks with a high short-term foreign borrowing position, imposing a levy on them, or alternatively, setting a position limit for currency spot and forward contracts.[29]

2.3.2 Protecting against Currency Rigging and Securing Market Integrity

It is widely accepted that price manipulating in the FX market is nearly impossible. Given that sophisticated professionals such as traders at the largest banks trade many trillions of dollars across the globe for 24 hours a day, it has been believed that any participants in the FX market could "not consistently generate excess returns by trading foreign exchanges".[30] However, such a firm belief broke down with the 2008 global financial crisis, and the *currency rigging* scandal which came to light in 2013 reaffirmed that foreign exchange markets are, contrary to common belief, neither so competitive nor that fair.[31]

Above all, a report by Bloomberg that uncovered all the rampant traders' misbehaviour in the market was a wake-up call indeed. On 12 June 2013, the international news agency revealed that "traders at some of the world's biggest banks manipulated benchmark foreign exchange rates used to set the value of trillions of dollars of investments", and some of them had been "front-running client orders".[32] Furthermore, such trading malpractices were reported to be already pervasive in the market for about ten years (see Table 3). The result

---

27 Jeanne and Korinek (2010), p 2.

28 For a detailed explanation of this mechanism of generating a crisis, see Korinek (2018).

29 On a related note, even the International Monetary Fund (IMF) that had long opposed to regulating cross-border capital flows changed its policy stance, and recognised the need for capital flow management especially in emerging market economies in the wake of the 2008 global financial crisis. See IMF (2012). For the subsequent development of arguments, see also IMF (2017).

30 Kang, *supra* n. 8, p 234.

31 Ibid.

32 Vaughan et al. (2013).

was tremendous. Immediately after the press release, regulators of the largest foreign exchange centres, including the UK Financial Conduct Authority (FCA) and the US Department of Justice (DOJ) initiated a probe into potential manipulation, which "has resulted in about $11.8 billion in fines for the largest global banks (e.g., Citi, Barclays, JP Morgan, Deutsche Bank), with another $2.3 billion spent to compensate customers and investors".[33] Moreover, not a few traders were "fired, suspended, or put on leave" and an employee of the Bank of England (BoE) was "dismissed for suspicion of exchange rate manipulation condonation and leakage of confidential customer information".[34] Most recently, on 16 May 2019, the EC "fined five lenders $1.2 billion(€1.07 billion) for their roles in FX cartels".[35]

The way traders obtained ill gotten profits from market manipulation was too simple (see Figure 2). By "sharing information on customers' orders, prices applicable to specific transactions, and open risk positions in different currencies via online invitation-only chat rooms, traders colluded in effort to place

TABLE 3 Timeline of the global currency rigging scandal

As of		Events
2005	July	– The first meeting of the Bank of England's FX Joint Standing Committee's chief dealers sub-group. These get-togethers between top London-based FX traders and senior BoE officials will become known as the chief dealers meetings. They will be held regularly every year up to 2013, where the traders and Bank officials will discuss market trends and issues. Every meeting will be chaired by BoE chief dealer Martin Mallett.
2006	July	– Minutes of a chief dealers meeting say the group discussed "evidence of attempts to move the market around popular fixing times by players that had no particular interest in that fix. It was noted that 'fixing business' generally was becoming increasingly fraught due to this behaviour".

33 Kang, *supra* n. 8, p 237.

34 Ibid.

35 Ibid.

TABLE 3 Timeline of the global currency rigging scandal (*cont.*)

As of		Events
2008	March to July	– A meeting of the BoE's FX Joint Standing Committee's chief dealers sub-group discusses the suggestion "that using a snapshot of the market may be problematic, as it could be subject to manipulation", BoE minutes say. Minutes of a meeting of the FX chief dealers say there was "considerable discussion" on the benchmark "fixings" again. The Federal Reserve Bank of New York makes enquiries into concerns surrounding benchmark Libor interest rates, sharing its analysis and suggestions for reforms with "the relevant authorities in the UK".
2012	April	– As the Libor scandal reaches its zenith, the regular FX chief dealers meeting included a "brief discussion on extra levels of compliance that many bank trading desks were subject to when managing client risks around the main set piece benchmark fixings", BoE minutes say.
2013	February	– The chief dealers group meets for what will be the last time.
	June	– Bloomberg News reports dealers used electronic chatrooms to share client order information to manipulate benchmark exchange rates at the 4:00 PM London "fixing". These chatrooms had names such as "The 3 Musketeers" and "The Cartel".
	July	– A scheduled chief dealers meeting for July 4 never takes place.
	September	– Swiss bank UBS provides the US Department of Justice with information on FX allegations in the hope of gaining antitrust immunity if charged with wrongdoing.
	October	– The investigation goes global. The DOJ, Britain's Financial Conduct Authority and Bank of England, and Switzerland's market regulator all open probes. The Hong Kong Monetary Authority says it is cooperating.
	December	– Several banks, including JP Morgan Chase, Goldman Sachs and Deutsche Bank ban traders from multi-dealer electronic chatrooms.

TABLE 3 Timeline of the global currency rigging scandal (*cont.*)

As of		Events
2014	January	– Citi fires chief dealer Rohan Ramchandani, a member of the BoE-chaired chief dealers group and the first trader in the unfolding scandal to be sacked.
	February	– The Financial Stability Board, the world's top financial regulator which coordinates policy for the G20, says it will review FX fixings. – New York's banking regulator opens its investigation.
	March	– The Bank of England suspends Martin Mallett, and appoints Lord Anthony Grabiner to lead an independent investigation into what the Bank knew of alleged currency market collusion and manipulation.
	July	– Britain's Serious Fraud Office formally opens investigation into FX rigging.
	November	– British and US authorities fine six of the world's biggest banks – Citi, JP Morgan, HSBC, RBS, UBS and Bank of America Merrill Lynch – a total of $4.3 billion for failing to prevent their traders sharing clients' order information and attempting to manipulate the market. – The Bank of England fires chief dealer Martin Mallett, and announces it has scrapped the regular chief dealers meetings for good.
	December	– Former RBS trader Paul Nash is the first individual to be arrested.
2015	May	– The US DOJ fines six banks (Citi, JP Morgan, HSBC, RBS, Barclays and Bank of America Merrill Lynch) a total of $6 billion. The first five pleaded guilty to felony charges, while BAML was fined for compliance failures.
	November	– Ex-Citi trader Perry Stimpson wins his unfair dismissal hearing at an employment tribunal in London.
2016	March	– Britain's SFO closes its FX investigation without having brought any charges, saying "the alleged conduct, even if proven and taken at its highest, would not meet the evidential test required to mount a prosecution for an offence contrary to English law".

TABLE 3 Timeline of the global currency rigging scandal (*cont.*)

As of		Events
2017	January	– US Department of Justice indicts three London-based former traders and members of "The Cartel" chatroom, Rohan Ramchandani, Richard Usher and Chris Ashton. Former Barclays trader Jason Katz becomes the first person to admit criminal wrongdoing in the FX probe, pleading guilty to US charges to participating in a price-fixing conspiracy.

Note: This timeline was compiled by a market columnist Jamie McGeever at Reuters.
SOURCE: MCGEEVER (2017)

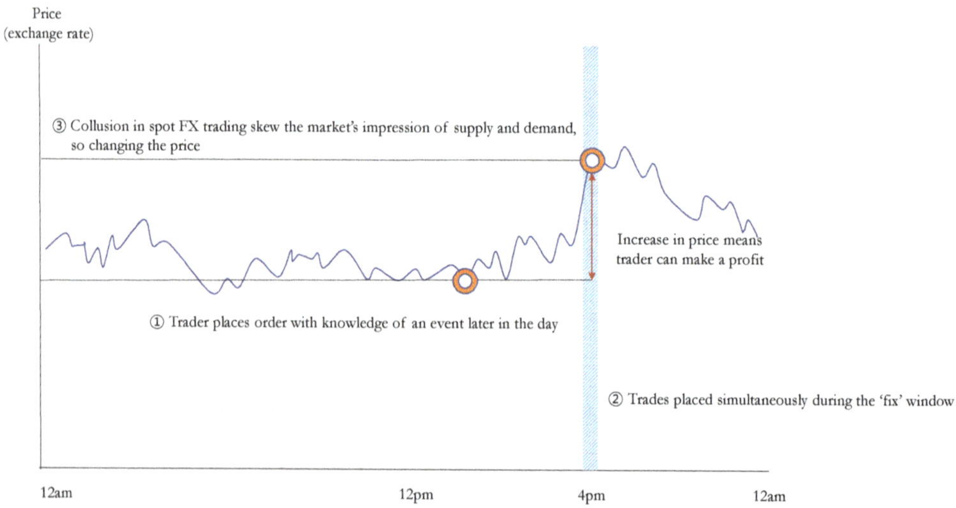

FIGURE 2 A typical pattern of FX benchmark (WMR 4 PM *fix*) manipulation
SOURCE: CHRISPIN (2015) (FROM "RETHINKING SPOT FX REGULATION", PUBLISHED ON WWW.TANDFONLINE.COM. REPRODUCED AND REPUBLISHED WITH PERMISSION. ALL RIGHTS RESERVED).

their orders aggressively over a very short period of time (e.g., just one minute)", thereby distorting the market prices (in this case, FX benchmark rate of World Market/Reuters (WMR) 4 PM London *fix*).[36]

36 Ibid., pp 237–238. World Market/Reuters (WMR) 4 PM London *fix* indicates the "FX benchmark rate which is daily calculated by the WM company, based on transactional and

Considering the fact that exchange rates can be manipulated, regulating the FX market is both reasonable and justifiable.[37] In fact, a host of FX derivative contracts such as currency forward/futures, option and swap are subject to the statutory regulation that governs all these types of transactions of financial instruments in all major jurisdictions. For example, the Commodity Exchange Act (CEA) enables the US governmental agency called the Commodities Futures Trading Commission (CFTC) to regulate and supervise unfair trading in the FX derivatives market.[38] Moreover, the Dodd-Frank Wall Street Reform and Consumer Protection Act (commonly referred to as Dodd-Frank) enacted in 2010 in the aftermath of the 2008 global financial crisis reinforced the regulation of over-the-counter (OTC) transactions related to FX derivatives, including a clearing obligation through an authorised or recognised central counterparty (CCP) and a mandatory reporting of derivatives transactions to swap data repositories (SDRS).[39] In particular, the Dodd-Frank Act has granted a broad regulatory authority that is comparable to the general anti-fraud provision of SEC Rule 10b–5 to the CFTC.[40]

The way the EU authority regulates the market is the ditto. FX derivatives are considered as financial instruments that are within the scope of the EU regulatory system, that is, Markets in Financial Instruments Directive (MiFID) and Market Abuse Regulation (MAR). Market manipulation for financial instruments is strictly prohibited, and in particular, MiFID II that entered into force on 3 January 2018 has implemented the post-trade reporting obligations (as close to real time as possible) for FX derivatives in order to enhance market

quoted data from actual currency deals that take place in a one-minute window around 4 PM London time (specifically, 3:59:30–4:00:30)". For a detailed procedure to produce the WMR *fix*, See FSB (2014).

37 Powers (2016), p 193.

38 Tormey (1997), pp 2327–2328. However, it is worth noting that the Commodities Futures Modernisation Act of 2000 rendered the CFTC unable to exercise its authority to OTC trading between the sophisticated parties. Some commentators contend that such radical deregulation was one of main reasons that the 2008 global financial crisis broke out. For the related arguments, see Stout (2011).

39 US Treasury Department (2012).

40 17 CFR §180 (2011). With regard to market manipulation, the CEA sets out four elements to constitute a violation of law; (i) manipulative act, (ii) intent, (iii) causation, (iv) artificial price, and, among other things, the fourth one, that is, a showing that market prices are determined by any factors other than the unfettered forces of supply and demand is the *sine que non*. Moreover, noteworthy here is that a mere attempt to manipulate the market may also constitute a crime. See Powers, *supra* n. 37, p 163.

transparency.[41] Similarly, the UK Financial Services and Markets Act (and the subsequent Financial Services Act of 2012) enables the UK authority (FCA) to regulate and supervise market abuse behaviours in transactions involving FX derivatives.

However, contrary to FX derivatives contracts, spot FX trading (that usually results in actual delivery within two business days) is not, if ever, statutorily regulated, but instead relies heavily on self-regulation. This is largely because of the conventional view that currency transactions occur in the most efficient and competitive market, and trading among the most sophisticated players in a highly regulated banking industry needs little governmental protection. In addition, most countries concern that the competitiveness of their FX markets may deteriorate when spot transactions are statutorily regulated.[42] Thus, regulators in every jurisdiction do not classify spot FX contracts into "financial (investment) instruments" that must address burdensome regulatory challenges, merely focusing on their function that serves the purpose of international payments and facilitates cross-border trades. Indeed, the EU MiFID II excludes spot FX contracts from a full list of "financial instruments" that are subject to the EU law, and the UK government also does not define spot FX contracts as qualifying "specified investments" that should meet various statutory and regulatory requirements.[43] As a consequence, spot FX is not today falling within the scope of the formal regulations, as a senior officer at the FCA once commented as follows:

> Spot FX sits in an interesting place on what we call our regulatory perimeter. Spot FX trading is only within the perimeter in certain circumstances, for example where a spot trade is ancillary to a transaction in a regulated 'financial instrument' (for example, when buying currency to purchase a bond), or where manipulation of prices on spot FX markets impacts the prices on regulated markets such as those for FX derivatives, or impacts on a benchmark. Most other FX trading is, in formal terms, outside our perimeter.[44]

---

41 See ESMA (2015). MiFID II mandated pre-trade report disclosure of information, such as bid/offer prices and the market depth at those prices, and post-trade report of transactional details (within 15 minutes after a transaction, and within 5 minutes from the year 2020) for financial instruments. However, FX derivatives were tentatively exempt from pre-trade reporting obligations because it deemed "illiquid assets" due to the lack of reliability of transactional data.

42 Powers, *supra* n. 37, pp 174–176.

43 See Financial Services and Markets Act 2000 (Regulated Activities) Order 2001 and amendment order thereof 2017.

44 See FCA (2016).

As referred above, however, the 2013 global currency rigging scandal made all market participants reconsider the current regulatory regime. Recognising that there is a nonnegligible defect in the existing FX legal system, many governments strived to improve their spot FX regulations, including filling the regulatory void. Additionally, the foreign exchange committee that consists of representatives of major financial institutions engaged in foreign currency trading in eight regions (Australia, Canada, ECB, Hong Kong, London, New York, Singapore, Tokyo) made a suggestion for the best market practice

TABLE 4 Key principles of the Global FX Code

Categories	Leading principles
Ethics	– Market Participants are expected to behave in an ethical and professional manner to promote the fairness and integrity of the FX Market.
Governance	– Market Participants are expected to have a sound and effective governance framework to provide for clear responsibility for and comprehensive oversight of their FX Market activity and to promote responsible engagement in the FX Market.
Execution	– Market Participants are expected to exercise care when negotiating and executing transactions in order to promote a robust, fair, open, liquid, and appropriately transparent FX Market.
Information Sharing	– Market Participants are expected to be clear and accurate in their communications and to protect Confidential Information to promote effective communication that supports a robust, fair, open, liquid, and appropriately transparent FX Market.
Risk management and Compliance	– Market Participants are expected to promote and maintain a robust control and compliance environment to effectively identify, manage, and report on the risks associated with their engagement in the FX Market.
Confirmation and Settlement	– Market Participants are expected to put in place robust, efficient, transparent, and risk-mitigating post-trade processes to promote the predictable, smooth, and timely settlement of transactions in the FX Market.

SOURCE: GFXC (2017)

on March 2015, and the Bank for International Settlements (BIS) made public the *Global FX Code* based on this in May 2017. The Code that is "a set of principles of good practice for foreign exchange market participants" provides key recommendations for compliance while doing FX business, "aiming to promote the integrity and effective functioning of the wholesale foreign exchange market".[45]

Moreover, automated algorithmic trading to counteract traders' arbitrary execution of orders has become popular in the market, and the time window during which WMR 4 PM *fix* is daily calculated has widened from one minute to five minutes to discourage the opportunistic behaviours of traders.[46]

Notwithstanding such efforts to improve market practices and trading cultures, however, more recent studies point out that the effectiveness of enhancing self-regulation or of just reinforcing internal controls is limited, and that spot FX trading should be statutorily regulated. For example, according to the Bank of England (BoE), the FX market still lends itself to "conflicts of interests; limited transparency; poor benchmark design; market concentration; and a reduction in the effectiveness of market discipline".[47] Apparently, banks have "intentionally disregarded the industry's best practices" and thus even new internal systems will not be enough to deter and prevent misconduct. Indeed, regulators argue that codes of ethics or conduct do "not supplant the government regulation, but complement it".[48] On a related note, after a comprehensive and thorough review of FX conduct risk, the UK authorities (HM Treasury, Bank of England, Financial Conduct Authority) proposed the following regulatory actions; (i) recordkeeping of transactional details of those who engage in FX businesses, (ii) mandatory reporting of suspicious transactions to the authorities, (iii) an application of market abuse regulation to spot FX trading.[49] However, these recommendations were not implemented. Instead, the regulator tried to substantiate and reinforce an existing self-regulation programme (so-called "FX remediation programme"), in which around 30 banks and financial institutions that currently trade over 70% of FX transactions in

45 The detailed information of the Global FX code is available at https://www.bis.org/about/factmktc/fx_global_code.htm.

46 To be sure, banks are increasingly turning to algorithmic trading to execute currency orders. Reportedly, "algorithms are now used to carry out roughly 90% of orders placed at the daily *fix* rate, compared with about 5% before the FX rigging scandal". See Albanese (2015).

47 An independent review by the Bank has found that "market discipline was either lacking or non-existent in FX". See Powers, *supra* n. 37, pp 179–180.

48 See Potter (2015).

49 See HM Treasury et al. (2015).

the UK market take part. The FCA has here required covered institutions to embed the Global FX Code prepared by the BIS into their internal control systems and has regularly examined the status of FX conduct risk, which includes a conflict of interest with customers, compensation and governance of FX businesses, and a strict ban of trading collusion, and manipulation of benchmark rate (*fix*).[50] However, admittedly, as this programme is a self-regulation at the very most, it is not legally enforced.

Meanwhile, the European Securities and Markets Authority (ESMA) proceeded with the consultation with respect to extending MAR to spot FX trades, but has concluded that "it is necessary to perform further analysis once the revision of the FX Global Code has been finalised".[51] This European stance is reminiscent of a former governor of the Bank of England, Mark Carney's earlier mention that "a failure to establish effective common standards that are adhered to would likely result in more restrictive regulation".[52] This message is what the US Fed also emphasised. Taken together, regulators around the world are seemingly yet reluctant to impose strict conduct regulations on FX businesses and let the market regulated as lightly as possible. However, it should be noted that we always "carry the risk of a recurrence of the 2013 manipulation scandal, absent any fundamental reform to the current regulatory system".[53]

3 Current Landscape of the Korean FX Law and Regulations

3.1 *An Overview of the Regulatory System*

The governing law that regulates every transaction in the Korean foreign exchange market is the Foreign Exchange Transactions Act (FETA). However, the FETA merely provides general principles in a fairy broad manner, and the Foreign Exchange Transactions Regulation (FETR) promulgated by the finance minister thereunder sets forth a host of specific rules. The Korean FX law defines its regulatory scope as follows.[54]

50 Apart from this, the UK government introduced a new provision of benchmarks regulation into the Financial Services and Markets Act of 2000, prohibiting manipulative practices in markets determining several key reference rates (such as SONIA, RONIA, LBMA Gold Price, LBMA Silver Price, WM/Reuters London 4 PM Closing Spot Rate, ICE Brent Index and ICE Swap Rate) in April 2015. See HM Treasury et al. (2016). After that, the UK benchmarks regulation was merged into the EU Benchmarks Regulation in February 2018.

51 See ESMA (2020).

52 See *supra* n. 48 (citing his speech at the Bank).

53 Kang, *supra* n. 8, p 234.

54 Art. 2 of the FETA.

- Foreign exchange in Korea, foreign exchange transactions conducted therein, or other acts related thereto;
- Transactions, payments or receipts between Korea and any foreign country, or other acts related thereto (including those which are performed in any foreign country and which have an effect in Korea);
- Transactions between an individual having a domicile or residence in a foreign country and a legal entity having a main office in a foreign country, which are denominated or payable in the currency of Korea, or other acts related thereto;
- Acts conducted by an individual having a domicile or residence in Korea, or his/her agents, employers or other employees in connection with his/her assets or business in a foreign country;
- Acts conducted by a representative, agents, employers or other employees of a legal entity having its main office in Korea in connection with assets or business of the legal entity in a foreign country.

Only qualified financial institutions (so-called "foreign exchange agencies") that are registered with the finance minister (the Ministry of Economy and Finance) are entitled to engage in a FX business "insofar as it is directly related to the core business of the institutions", but the Korean government also permitted a person who is not a financial institution (so-called "a specialised foreign exchange dealer") to operate some business that is related to money exchange and transfer by amending the Act in 2017.[55]

Moreover, any person who engages in FX transactions must report the transaction details to the authorities (Ministry of Economy and Finance, the Bank of Korea, or foreign exchange banks) in advance and should be able to submit evidence (i.e., the relevant information or documents), unless the FX law and regulations waive the obligation or state otherwise. Noteworthy here is that foreign exchange agencies that conduct a FX transaction with customers are obliged to "confirm whether transactions, payments or receipts of their customers are permitted or reported under the Act".[56] In particular, foreign exchange banks deal with most transactions, playing an important role in producing transactional data and information that can be used for the

55 Art. 8(1) to (3) of the FETA. Any person who intends to engage in a foreign exchange business and to register with the finance minister must meet the pre-set standards of "capital, facilities and professional human resources" sufficient to conduct such business.

56 Art. 10(1) of the FETA.

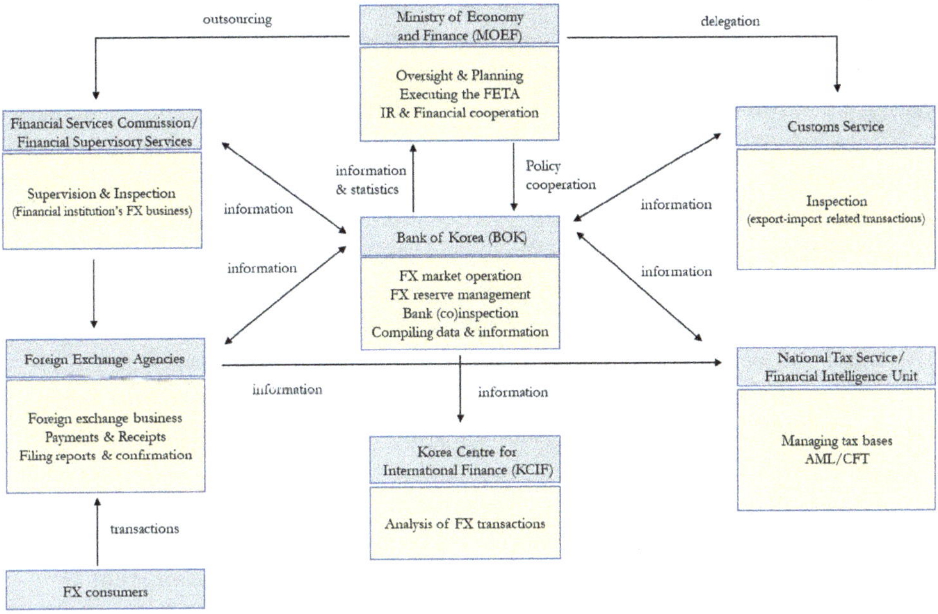

FIGURE 3 Foreign exchange system in Korea
SOURCE: BOK (2016)

governmental authorities to monitor the foreign exchange market and cross-border capital flows.[57]

Furthermore, the FETA designates the Bank of Korea as "an institution to relay, concentrate, exchange data on foreign exchange transactions, payments or receipts".[58] This is to reinforce monitoring of international capital flows in normal times, enabling the government to take prompt policy actions in times of crisis. In addition, for some transactions that demand the post-trades management or surveillance (including foreign deposit, foreign currency borrowing, foreign direct investment (FDI), acquisition of overseas property), the finance minister mandates a person to engage in transactions with only a single designated (branch of) foreign exchange bank.[59]

57 For this reason, any bank employee "in charge of the business is deemed a public official in the application of the penal provisions under the Criminal Act or other Acts". See Art. 23 of the FETA.

58 Art. 25(2) of the FETA and Art. 39(1) of its enforcement decree.

59 Art. 10–11 of the FETR.

3.2 *A Brief History of the Regulatory System*

The history of the Korean FX law dates back to the Japanese imperialism era of 1930s, when the colonial government of Japan enforced the pre-war Capital Flight Prevention Law to fight against currency speculation and exchange rate volatility in Japan and also in Korea that was under Japanese rule.[60] In those times, Japan struggled to stabilise the value of its currency (Japanese Yen, JPN). The exchange rate (JPN/USD) plummeted from $49 per 100 Yen (in December 1931) to $20 per 100 Yen (in September 1932) in less than a year. This was because the United States kept maintaining the "gold standard system" but Japan did not during the economic recession. As a response of market turmoil, the Japanese government introduced the tight capital control measures; (i) prohibiting currency speculation, (ii) controlling export of gold, (iii) requiring permission from the government when investing in foreign securities, (iv) controlling no-draft export. In doing so, the Japanese FX authority intended to restrict every international transaction other than exceptionally permitted one.[61] Such a strict and centralised control system of foreign exchange remained the same under the United States army military government after liberation in 1945.

However, as exports grew at a rapid pace and foreign capital inflows gradually increased in 1960s, the Korean government recognised the need to efficiently and effectively allocate foreign currencies collected, which led to the first enactment of the Korean FX law, that is, the Foreign Exchange Control Act (FECA). In enacting the FECA (Act no. 933, in December 1961), the Korean government established the rule of "ban in principle and permission only in exception" (so-called positive regulation system) in order to plan and budget foreign funds into the most productive part of the economy in the nascent stage of economic development.

The Korean government overhauled its FX law and regulations in the wake of the 1997 Asian financial crisis, focusing on deregulation of exchange rate system and capital control measures. In fact, even before the crisis, regulations had been gradually eased due to the need for expanding foreign exchange transactions driven by rapid trade and economic growth.[62] Nonetheless, it is

60 Seo (2018), pp 209–210.

61 Ibid., p 217.

62 For example, Korea notified acceptance of Article VIII obligations required by the IMF, such as "avoidance of restrictions on current payments, avoidance of discriminatory currency practices, Convertibility of foreign-held balances". Additionally, the Korean government pursued various financial liberalisation policies in 1990s, including allowance of foreign investment in shares of companies listed on the Korea Stock Exchange.

TABLE 5 Evolution of the exchange rate bands

Effective dates	Mar. 2, 1990	Sep. 2 1991	July 1, 1992	Oct. 1 1993	Nov. 1, 1994	Dec. 1, 1995	Nov. 20, 1997	Dec. 16, 1997
Band width (%)	±0.4	±0.6	±0.8	±1.0	±1.5	±2.25	±10.0	Abolished

SOURCE: BOK (2016)

through the repeal and replacement of the FECA with the Foreign Exchange Transactions Act in 1998 (Act no. 5550, entry into force on 1 April 1999) that fundamental changes occurred. With the enactment of the FETA, the exchange rate system has fully transitioned to the floating regime (see Table 5), and the Korean government has embarked upon a string of policies and plans for the foreign exchange market liberalisation as shown in Table 6.

As a consequence, FX regulations have been considerably eased. The overall regulatory framework has changed into the negative regulation system (i.e., "permission in principle and ban only in exception"), and both individuals and corporates today are able to engage in FX transactions with even lesser restrictions than under the old FECA regime.

Meanwhile, the Korean government set forth a roadmap for regulatory reform that consists of the following policy tasks: (i) improve procedures of international payments/receipts, (ii) exempt pre-trades reporting obligations for capital transactions, (iii) repeal the obligation to residents holding claims against non-residents to collect the claims back to Korea, (iv) ease regulations regarding FDI and acquisition of overseas real property, (v) expand the scope of FX businesses of nonbank financial institutions, (vi) introduce new types of FX business in the market, (vii) reinforce competent authorities' monitoring and analytical capacity, (viii) improve the efficacy of prudential regulations, (ix) enforce stricter rules (of punishment/penalties) on offenders.[63] Out of these, the Korean government has tentatively completed the tasks (iii), (vi), (viii), and (ix) to date. Specifically, the provision that "requires resident creditors to collect and recover debts owed by non-resident debtors and to retrieve them to Korea" was abolished, and a new type of business called "specialised foreign exchange dealer" was introduced. In addition, the authorities

63 MOEF (2015).

implemented the foreign currency liquidity coverage ratio (LCR) into their regulatory toolbox, and the offenders now face more severe punishment.[64]

On July 2022, the Korean government further announced the enactment of the "New Foreign Exchange Act (whose title is yet provisional)". Although the government did not set forth any concrete or detailed provisions, the FX authority (Ministry of Economy and Finance) stressed a need for fundamental reform of the existing legal system in response to structural changes in an economy (e.g., population aging and declining potential growth) and investor preference for overseas financial assets. Thus, the finance minister came up with a plan to repeal and replace the current FETA, and to this end, it declared the governmental support for the proposals to deregulate considerably – specifically, the MOEF reaffirmed plans to abolish the pre-trades reporting system with minimal exceptions, and to extend the FX business opportunities for nonbank financial institutions to operate, adopting the principle of "same activity, same regulation". Moreover, the government set out its plan to improve the architecture, language, and accessibility of the statute, while possibly avoiding the problem of excessive delegation of legislative authority to the executive branch.[65]

TABLE 6 A string of FX liberalisation reforms after the 1997 Asian financial crisis

Actions	Details
1st FX liberalisation plan (April 1999)	– Repeal the "non-speculative demand principle" of FX forward – Allow corporates to borrow short-term foreign funds and abolish their most international payment restrictions – Shift from authorisation system to registration system in relation to FX businesses
2nd FX liberalisation plan (January 2001)	– Abolish individuals' most international payment restrictions – Deregulate residents' opening foreign (currency) deposit and non-residents' opening domestic (the Korean Won, KRW) short-term deposit account

64 For example, by amending the penalty provisions in 2017, the maximum imprisonment with labour extended from three years to five years and the maximum fine also increased from three hundred million won to five hundred million won (see Art. 27 of the FETA).

65 MOEF (2022).

TABLE 6 A string of FX liberalisation reforms after the 1997 Asian financial crisis (*cont.*)

Actions	Details
Promoting outward investment (June 2005)	– Abolish corporates' limit (per item) to investment on foreign financial businesses – Extend the limit of individuals' FDI from $1million to $3million – Extend the limit of individuals' acquisition of real estate abroad from $300,000 to $500,000
FX liberalisation propel (May 2006)	– Extend the limit of non-residents' KRW borrowing from 1billion won to 10billion won – Extend the limit of export or import of KRW (with possession) from $10,000 to $1million – Allow residents to invest in foreign real estate (up to $1million)
FX system improvement plan (November 2007)	– Abolish the residents' investment limit of foreign real estate – Permit postal services and saving bank (thrift institutions) to engage in money exchange business.
New macroprudential FX policies (June/November 2010)	– Set limits for FX forward positions of domestic banks and branches of foreign banks – Impose bank levies (so called "macroprudential stability levy") on non-core funding
Easing FX transactions regulation (July 2014)	– Extend the limit of international payments/receipts that does not require foreign exchange banks' confirmation from $1,000 to $2,000 – Extend the limit of funds transfer (such as capital transactions, set-offs, and the third-party payments/receipts) that is exempt from pre-trades reporting from $1,000 to $2,000 – Repeal pre-trade transactions reporting of FDI up to $500,000 and replace it with post-trade transactions reporting
FX transactions regulation reform (June 2015)	– Repeal the obligation to residents holding claims against non-residents to collect the claims back to Korea, leaving it for just emergency use – Adopt the "negative" regulation system of FX businesses; that is, allow financial institutions to engage in FX businesses in principle, forbidding them in exceptional circumstances that the FX law defines.

TABLE 6 A string of FX liberalisation reforms after the 1997 Asian financial crisis (*cont.*)

Actions	Details
Introducing foreign currency liquidity coverage ratio (LCR) (January 2017)	– Require banks to meet the foreign currency liquidity coverage ratio (LCR)
Further easing FX regulation (July 2017)	– Extend the limit of international payments/receipts that does not require foreign exchange banks' confirmation from \$2,000 to \$3,000 – Permit a qualified "specialised foreign exchange dealer" who is not a financial institution to engage in money exchange and transfer business

Note: In 2019, the Korean government extended the limit of international payments/receipts that does not require foreign exchange banks' confirmation from \$3,000 to \$5,000.
SOURCE: MOEF (2018)

3.3 *Policy Framework and Strategies*

Article 1 of the FETA expressly states that the Act aims to "contribute to the sound development of the national economy by striving to facilitate foreign transactions, to maintain equilibrium in the balance of payments and to stabilise the value of currency *by ensuring liberalisation of foreign exchange transactions and of other foreign transactions, and by invigorating market function*". This is in contrast to the same provision (Article 1) of the FECA, which stipulated that the purpose of the Act is to "contribute to the sound development of the national economy by harmonising foreign transactions, striving for international balance of payments and stabilising the currency value *through rational regulation or control of foreign exchange, and domestic and foreign transactions thereof*".[66] That is, while the purpose of FX law and regulations remain the same, the way the authority pursues it has become different: the former emphasises the role of market, whereas the latter gave a priority to the government's control.

On a related note, Article 4(1) of the FETA provides that the finance minister should "strive to facilitate foreign exchange transactions and other foreign transactions by imposing restrictions under this Act to the minimum necessary extent". The following is a list of policy or regulatory measures currently

66 The FECA here refers to the Act no. 5040.

in operation by the Korean government. The FETA provides the legal basis for these institutional arrangements.

3.3.1 Ordinary Central Bank Intervention for FX Market Stabilisation

The finance minister should "endeavour to create a foundation for stable supply and demand for foreign exchange and to stabilise the foreign exchange market, and formulate policies therefor".[67] In practice, the international finance bureau of the Ministry of Economy of Finance formulates exchange rate policy, and the Bank of Korea enforces the policy in a way that intervenes in the FX market using foreign exchange reserves and the foreign exchange equalisation fund.[68] FX authorities typically "lean against the wind" of the market's pressure; that is, buying when there is excess selling pressure, and selling when there is excess buying pressure. In doing so, they ensure stability in the market, but it should be noted that the exchange rate policy targets its volatility, not a specified level.[69]

Aside from this, the finance minister "may determine the basic exchange rate, purchase and sale rate of foreign exchange, and arbitrated rate of exchange in foreign exchange transactions, if it is necessary for harmonious and orderly foreign exchange transactions".[70] However, taking into consideration of the legislative intent, this provision should not be read as being applicable in normal times, but can be invoked only in exceptional circumstances, such as a currency crisis.

3.3.2 Macroprudential Regulations for Capital Flow Management

Managing the volume and pace of cross-border capital flows is quite important for FX market stabilisation. We know all too well that currency crises

67 Art. 4(2) of the FETA.

68 The Bank of Korea "exercises an advisory function concerning the government's policies on exchange rates, the foreign currency loans and deposits of banking institutions, and the setting of foreign exchange overbought and oversold position limits on them" (see Article 83 of the Bank of Korea Act). The foreign exchange equalisation fund established as a fund under Article 5 of the National Finance Act is funded with (i) contributions and withholdings from the government, (ii) money raised by issuing foreign exchange equalisation fund bonds, (iii) withholdings or temporary loans from any foreign government, any foreign central bank, or other residents or non-residents, (iv) macroprudential stability levies and other financial resources, which can be used for market intervention by the central bank or relief loan provision during a crisis (see Article 13 of the FETA).

69 The Korean government stressed that "the exchange rate is normally determined in the market, and smoothing operation is done by the authority in both directions when there is excessive exchange rate volatility". See MOEF (2017).

70 Art. 5(1) of the FETA.

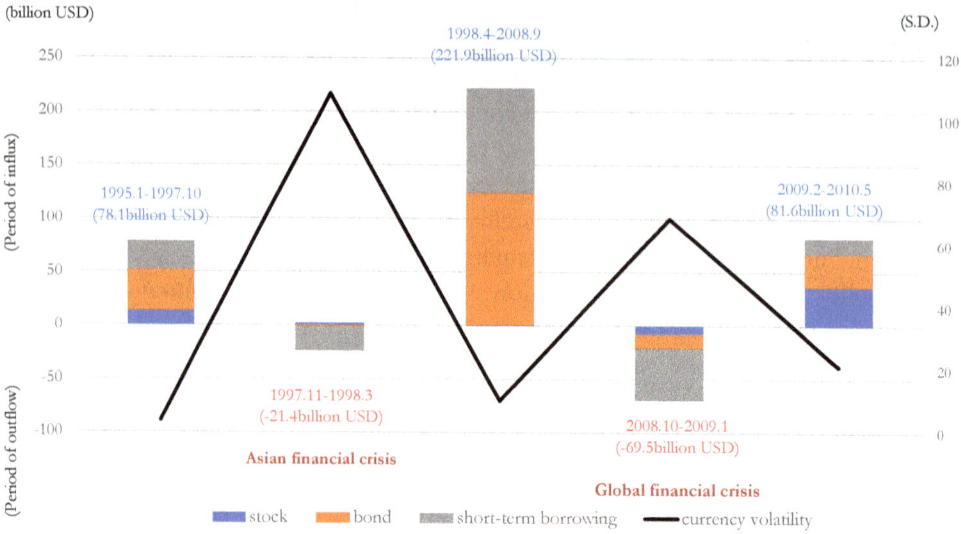

FIGURE 4 Foreign capital flows before and after crises
Note: Currency volatility is measured by the standard deviation (S.D.) of daily returns of USD/KRW exchange rate
SOURCE: MOEF (2010)

have frequently occurred since the 1990s, when financial liberalisation progressed significantly across the globe. In particular, those crises had patterns in common: that is, a large volume of foreign capital (especially in the form of short-term foreign borrowing) flows into the economy in the boom phase and abruptly outflows in bust phase, drying up foreign currency liquidity and hiking exchange rate volatility. The 1997 Asian financial crisis and the 2008 Global financial crisis are the typical examples (see Figure 4).

In 2010, the Korean government introduced new macroprudential policy measures (such as FX forward position limit, Macroprudential stability levy) to mitigate adverse effects of excessive foreign capital movements. They are prophylactic measures, in that the measures particularly aim at managing the volume and pace of the short-term external debt (or short-term foreign currency borrowing) to an adequate level so that it may not trigger a currency crisis when a sudden stop or capital flow reversals hit the economy.

FX forward position limit puts its legal grounds on Article 11(2) of the FETA, which states that "where it is deemed necessary for maintaining stability in the foreign exchange market and soundness of foreign exchange agencies, the finance minister may impose necessary restrictions on the raising and operation of foreign currency, such as determining the asset-liability ratio of foreign currency by foreign exchange agencies". This regulation was implemented due to reflection that banks' long position in FX forward markets, which surged prior to the outbreak of the 2008 global financial crisis, served as a path to significantly increase short-term external debt and to amplify systemic risk in the whole financial markets. In actuality, it was estimated that about half of the increase in total external debt from 2006 to 2007 just before the crisis was driven by the banking sector's increased positioning in FX forward market.[71] The Korean government found that this was mainly because shipbuilders and asset managers had taken large short positions in currency forward market, and the banks that had taken long positions as counterparties increased short-term foreign currency borrowing to sell them in spot FX market: that is, banks squared their positions to hedge currency risk. The FX authority hereby set the FX forward position limit of 50% of equity capital for domestic banks and 250% of equity capital for foreign bank branches, and has adjusted it upwards or downwards depending on market conditions.

Macroprudential stability levy (also known as bank levy) was implemented in August 2011 pursuant to Article 11–2 of the FETA. In a nascent stage, the regulation targeted only banks, but it also covered securities companies, insurers, and financial companies specialising in loan business in 2015, when nonbank financial institutions' business scope of foreign exchange expanded. The levy is imposed on noncore (or non-deposit) foreign currency liabilities (within one-year maturity) held by domestic and foreign banks, and chargeable rate is currently set at 10bp.

3.3.3 Capital Controls Measures for Emergency Preparedness

The finance minister may exercise various emergency plans, such as (temporary) suspension of FX transactions during a crisis to pursuant of Article 6 of the FETA (see Table 7).[72] These measures are to protect national interests when the market environment may cause, or threaten to cause serious injury to the economy and the whole domestic industry. However, the Korean government has not exercised the safeguard measures even during the past currency crises

71 See MOEF (2010).

72 With respect to the imposition of obligation to residents holding claims against non-residents to collect the claims back, the finance minister could have "required resident creditors whose claims exceed the amount equivalent to $500,000 per item to collect and recover debts owed by non-resident debtors and to retrieve them to Korea within three years from the date of maturity or fulfilment of the condition therefor". However, the provision of the FETA (Article 7) and its enforcement decree (Article 12) were repealed with the amendment of the law in January 2017.

TABLE 7 Safeguard measures (Article 6 of the FETA)

Measures	Triggering events
Temporary suspension of payment, receipt or the whole or a part of transactions Imposition of an obligation to safekeep, deposit or sell means of payment or precious metals in or to the Bank of Korea, government agencies, the foreign exchange equalisation fund, or financial institutions. Imposition of obligation to residents holding claims against non-residents to collect the claims back to Korea.	– If such measures are deemed inevitable on account of the outbreak of natural calamities, wars, conflicts of arms, grave and sudden changes in domestic and foreign economic conditions, or other situations equivalent thereto.
Imposition of an obligation to obtain permission on any person who intends to perform capital transactions	– In a case where international payments and international finance are confronted or are liable to be confronted with serious difficulty.
Imposition of an obligation to deposit part of means of payment acquired in such transactions in the Bank of Korea, the foreign exchange equalisation fund or financial institutions on any person who performs capital transactions	– In a case where the movement of capital between Korea and a foreign country brings or is liable to bring on serious obstacles in carrying out currency policies, exchange rate policies and other macroeconomic policies.

Note: Measures above may be taken for a period not exceeding six months unless there exist special grounds to the contrary, and if reasons for such measures cease to exist, such measures must be cancelled without delay.

for fear that any form of capital controls will deteriorate the Korea economy's international credit standings.[73]

73 On a related note, the Korean authority may instead resort to the Article 8(5) of the FETA, which provides that "foreign exchange agency must obtain authorisation of the finance minister in concluding a contract concerning business subject to application of the Act with foreign financial institutions", if it is recognised by the finance minister as necessary to "pay careful attention to the inflow and outflow of foreign exchange as it is likely to cause serious harm to the national economy due to a sudden instability in international financial markets (Article of 16(6) of the enforcement decree of the Act)".

3.3.4 Regulation and Supervision of Foreign Exchange Agencies

In order to operate a FX business, a foreign exchange agency must "prepare capital, facilities and professional human resources sufficient to conduct such business and register it with the finance minister in advance" (Article 8(1) of the FETA).[74] More specifically, the enforcement decree of the Act provides that (i) "its capital size and financial structure must be adequate in light of criteria for financial soundness applied to the relevant financial companies", (ii) it must be "connected with the foreign exchange information concentration agency (in this case, the Bank of Korea) by means of a computer network that enables it to report every transactional data in time and it must also be equipped with data processing facilities for effective post-management", and (iii) it must "secure at least two persons for each business office, who have at least two years of experience in foreign exchange".[75]

Moreover, foreign exchange agencies must comply with conduct of business regulations that govern the conduct of financial institutions, such as managing conflicts of interest, promoting investor protections and market integrity. Specialised foreign exchange dealers who are not financial institutions but operate money exchange (or a small-amount overseas remittance) business are subject to rules that secure safety and reliability of transactions. For example, the finance minister may require specialised foreign exchange dealers to "deposit a performance bond (not less than 300 million won) in an institution (in this case, the Financial Supervisory Service) designated by the minister or purchasing an insurance policy or joining a mutual aid program".[76]

The Korean government recently implemented the new rules for market manipulating prohibitions. Against the backdrop of the 2013 global FX rigging scandal, recognising the need for statutorily regulating the market practices, a new Article 10(2) of the FETA was crafted in January 2017, and the government promulgated its enforcement decree (Article 20–2) to pursuant to this provision in June of the same year.[77] According to the new rules, it is prohibited

---

74 On a similar note, anyone who intends to provide foreign exchange brokerage services must prepare capital (paid-in capital not less than four billion won), facilities (equipped with computerised facilities for conducting foreign exchange affairs and reporting) and professional human resources (not less than two professionals having the capability necessary for conducting business) to conduct such business and obtain authorisation of the finance minister. See Article 9(1) of the FETA and Article 18(2) of its enforcement decree.

75 Art. 13(2) of enforcement decree of the FETA.

76 Art. 8(7) of the FETA and Art. 17(2) of its enforcement decree.

77 This newly adopted rule has significant meaning from the perspective of regulators and supervisors in that it is virtually the first attempt to statutorily regulate market abuse behaviours in the spot FX market in major jurisdictions. Prior to that, Seoul Foreign Exchange Committee (FXC), a self-regulatory organisation, regulated and supervised the

for any person to "conduct acts that undermine the integrity of FX market to gain unfair profit or to make a third party gain unfair profit", including "an act of changing or fixing the market price of any foreign exchange", and "an act that unfairly affects or is likely to unfairly affect foreign exchange rates" by wrongful conducts (such as entering matched orders, disseminating rumours or devising stratagems in falsehood).[78] Any person who violates this rule may be "punished by imprisonment with labour for not more than five years or by a fine not exceeding five hundred million won".[79]

In addition, the Korean government made a substantial revision to the existing FX prudential regulations in June 2016, with a special focus on enhancing resilience of financial institutions in a period of financial stress (see Table 8). The most important lesson from the 2008 global financial crisis is that financial institutions must reinforce short-term liquidity risk management. Of course, balance sheet management is important but we have observed that asset recovery rates or rollover rates unexpectedly plunged during a crisis, and the conventional (prudential) indicators lost explanatory or predictive power considerably. Indeed, banks met the regulatory standard of current assets/liabilities mismatch ratio that require them to maintain over 85% during the 2008 crisis, but faced the risk of impaired liquidity in the FX market.[80] The authority hereby implemented the foreign currency liquidity coverage ratio (LCR) regulation, requiring banks to hold sufficient high-quality liquid assets that can be immediately covered into cash with minimal or no loss of value (e.g., cash, central bank reserves, government securities), so that they may meet at least one month of foreign currency liquidity needs. If a bank fails to meet this standard, it must submit the statement of compliance to the regulator for the first two times, but the liquidity ratio rises by 5%p for each violation of the rule. When it violates the regulation five times or more, the bank may not borrow funds from any other lenders until it fulfils the requirement to satisfy the minimum threshold of the regulation. Besides, other regulations that were recognised by the government to overlap with the LCR regulation were abolished or much simplified.

---

business conduct of traders in the Korean FX market. The committee consists of 31 financial institutions, including six nationwide commercial banks, three specialised banks, two regional banks, twelve foreign banks branches, the Bank of Korea, the Korea Exchange.

78 Art. 10(2) of the FETA and Art. 20–2 of its enforcement decree.

79 Art. 27(1)(6) of the FETA. If the "triple value of the object related to the violation exceeds five hundred million won, the fine shall not be more than the triple value of such object".

80 Although current assets/liabilities mismatch ratio of banking sector in Korea declined slightly from 102.7% at the end of 2007 to 98.8% at the end of 2008, it still satisfied the required level of 85%. However, rollover rates of foreign borrowing plummeted from 126.4% in January 2008 to 39.9% in October of the same year, and accordingly many banks experienced the severe debt overhang problem. See MOEF (2016[b]).

TABLE 8 Coverage of prudential measures for foreign exchange risks in Korea

	Before	After
Position limit	Caps on overall (FX spot/forward) positions: 50% of owner's capital at the end of the previous month	Maintained
	Caps on FX forward positions: – Local banks: 30% – Foreign bank branches: 150%	Position limit extensions – Local banks: 40% – Foreign bank branches: 200%
Liquidity regulation	Foreign currency liquidity ratio (three months or less maturity): Current assets/current liabilities ≥ 85%	(Abolished)
	Maturity mismatch ration (gap ratio) – Terms to maturity of seven days: (assets – liabilities)/total foreign exchange claims ≥ -3% – Terms to maturity of one month: (assets – liabilities)/total foreign exchange claims ≥ –10%	Maturity mismatch ratio (gap ratio) – Terms to maturity of one month: (assets-liabilities)/total foreign exchange claims ≥ –10% Foreign currency liquidity coverage ratio: High quality liquid assets/one month net cash outflow ≥ 80% (by 2019)
	Net stable funding ratio (one year or more maturity, USD 50 million and above): Available amount of stable funding/required amount of stable funding ≥ 100%	Maintained
	Foreign currency high-quality liquid assets: – About 2% of total foreign exchange claims or – Maximum drawdown within two months	– (Abolished)

TABLE 8 Coverage of prudential measures for foreign exchange risks in Korea (*cont.*)

	Before	After
Macroprudential stability levy (Bank levy)	Chargeable rate (non-deposit foreign exchange liabilities of one year or less maturity): – banks 10bp – securities/insurance companies 5bp – When the weighted average maturity of non-deposit foreign exchange liabilities are – 2~3 years or less, 2bp – 3~4 years or less, 3bp – 4 years or more, 4bp deducted from above	Maintained
Others	To scrap the special tax exemption on foreign investment in government (or central bank) issued bonds: Revival of a 14% tax on interest income and a 20% tax on capital gains Restriction on foreign currency bank loans: For overseas use only	Maintained

Note: The revised rules have been effective since June 2016 except for the foreign currency liquidity coverage ratio (LCR), which was implemented in 2017.
SOURCE: KANG (2016)

3.3.5 Procedural Measures for Monitoring and Taking Prompt Actions

Any person who intends to conduct a FX transaction must report transactional details to the relevant authorities in advance. This rule applies to each step in the transaction. More specifically, anyone who engages in a capital transaction (including foreign deposit, trust, borrowing and lending, guarantee, securities issuance and acquisition, derivative contracts) is required to report it to the registered foreign exchange banks, the Bank of Korea, or MOEF prior to the transaction.[81] Among other things, "with respect to overseas direct investment, acquisition of overseas real estate or any right thereto by a resident", the finance minister "may examine the feasibility, such as whether an investor is qualified and the amount of investment is reasonable, and determine whether to accept such report".[82]

Moreover, when a resident makes settlement by using unconventional methods of payments or receipts, he or she must report, in advance, on the methods of such payments or receipts to the finance minister.[83] This is because "payment of the total amount through a foreign exchange agency, etc. for transactions between the parties" is a fundamental principle of foreign exchange settlements under the FETA. The Korean government thinks that those transactions may cause great difficulties monitoring cross-border movements of funds, and it therefore pays an enhanced regulatory attention to them. Consider a hypothetical example that a foreign employee working for a Korean company wants to send money to her family members living abroad. The foreign worker has transferred money via a currency dealer who is not officially registered with the finance minister, not going through a foreign exchange bank. Certainly, this is a breach of the FX law that prohibits any unregistered dealers from engaging in FX businesses (Article 8(1) of the FETA). Also, the sender of money has violated the law because he or she did not report on the method to the authority.[84]

---

81 Art. 18(1), (2) of the FETA. The FETA permits a court to discharge these offenders subject to criminal sanctions. Any person who fails to observe an obligation to report capital transactions may be "punished by imprisonment with labour for not more than one year or by a fine not exceeding one hundred million won", *provided* that the amount of violation (of an obligation to report) exceeds one billion won (Art. 29(1) of the Act and Art. 40(1) of its enforcement decree).

82 Art. 18(3) of the FETA.

83 Art. 16 of the FETA. The Act lists such types of method. They include (i) "when a resident makes any settlement by extinguishing or offsetting a claim or liabilities by means of balancing, (ii) when he or she makes any settlement after one year, (iii) when a resident pays or receives money to or from a person who is not a party to the transaction in question, or a resident who is not a party to the transaction in question pays or receives money to or from a non-resident who is a party thereto, (iv) when he or she pays or receives money without going through a foreign exchange agency or specialised foreign exchange dealers".

84 These offenders are subject to criminal charges. Unregistered dealers may be "punished by an imprisonment with labour for not more than three years or by a fine not exceeding three hundred million won" (Article 27–2 of the Act), and the sender of money may be "punished by imprisonment with labour for not more than one year or by a fine not exceeding one hundred million won", provided that the amount of violation (of an

Furthermore, the FX law provides that the finance minister "may require a resident or non-resident who intends to export or import any means of payment or securities whose amount exceeds ten thousand dollars to file a report to the Customs Service".[85] Of course, if the original transaction or method has already been reported to the authorities, the person who exports the payment instrument may be exempt from such an additional reporting obligation.

When a person remits the payment or take receipt via a foreign exchange agency (mostly a foreign exchange bank), he or she must submit the documentary evidence and the agency should confirm that the person has fulfilled an obligation to report the original transaction.[86] A payment exceeding five thousand dollars per item is subject to this regulation, and a receipt is applicable to this rule when the amount exceeds fifty thousand dollars on the same day/the same person basis.[87]

In addition, any person who intends to conduct a FX transaction must be given a permission from the finance minister (or the Bank of Korea that is given its authority) "when it is inevitable for the faithful fulfilment of treaties concluded by Korea, and of generally recognised international laws and regulations", or "when it is necessary for especially contributing to international endeavour for the maintenance of international peace and security".[88] This is to ban FX transactions of "persons subject to restrictions on financial transactions" who are designated for the reason that they are involved in activities jeopardising the public interest (e.g., terrorism).[89]

---

obligation to report) exceeds 2.5 billion won (Article 29(1) of the Act and Article 40(1) of its enforcement decree).

85 Art. 17 of the FETA, Art. 31 of its enforcement decree, and Art. 6–2 of the FETR.

86 Art. 10(1) of the FETA.

87 Art. 4–2, 4–3 of the FETR. The authority does not impose an obligation to submit any supporting documents for a payment less than five thousand dollars per item, and only requires the verbal confirmation of a foreign exchange bank up to annual cumulative amount of fifty thousand dollars.

88 Art. 15 of the FETA.

89 On a similar note, the Act on Prohibition against the Financing of Terrorism and Proliferation of Weapons of Mass Destruction provides that the Financial Services Commission requires a person designated and publicly announced as a person subject to restrictions on financial transactions to obtain a permit from the Commission (or the Bank of Korea that is given its authority) when he or she intends to engage in financial transactions in the following cases: (i) "where restriction on the proliferation of weapons of mass destruction is necessary to comply with treaties to which Korea is a party, or generally accepted international laws in good faith, (ii) where restriction on the proliferation of weapons of mass destruction, etc. is necessary to especially contribute to international efforts to sustain international peace and security".

Meanwhile, some capital transactions, such as overseas direct investment, real property acquisition, which do not end with one-off, are subject to the post-trades reporting obligations during the term of a contract. This is to check whether the transaction has actually been made as originally reported and manage it afterwards. To this end, the government requires a person who engages in such a transaction to submit the interim report to a designated foreign exchange bank.

4 Central Problems in the Korean FX Regulatory System: A Critical Review and Analysis

4.1 *Operation of the Legal System Centred on Strict Administrative Procedure Regulations*

4.1.1 Identifying the Key Issues

Any person who intends to conduct a FX transaction, as previously discussed in detail, should fulfil his or her reporting obligations in advance. Without prior notice of transactions to the authorities, the person cannot proceed with subsequent transactions. This is to enable the government to closely monitor and control as many transactions as possible, which may contribute to mitigating risk as to illicit overseas transfers and to making the authorities take prompt actions against abrupt capital flow reversals. However, it is also undeniable that there are some defects that likely hinder the FX law from successfully achieving its policy objectives.

First, a party to the transactions can be subject to multiple reporting regulations on a step-by-step basis even when he or she engages in a single FX transaction, which must be quite onerous from the standpoint of the party. Further, such regulatory burden becomes not only an obstacle to facilitating transactions, but also raises some constitutional issues in that it imposes criminal sanctions on those who violate the rules. Consider that there is an importer who wants to pay in person for imported goods directly to a foreign exporter (that is, without sending money via a bank account). The importer must file an import declaration with customs under the Foreign Trade Act and Customs Act, and then report the payment methods (i.e., payment not going through a foreign exchange bank) to the Bank of Korea (Article 16 of the FETA), or otherwise report on export of means of payment to customs service (Article 17 of the FETA).[90] If the amount of money in question is relatively small, a rather light

90 Current transactions such as merchandise trades (i.e., import and export of goods) are not subject to the FETA, but are subject to the Foreign Trade Act or the Customs Act.

measure such as a warning will be taken, but if the amount that is in violation of Article 16 of the FETA exceeds 2.5 billion won, or if the amount that is in violation of Article 17 of the FETA exceeds $30,000, the offender will be "punished by imprisonment with labour for not more than one year or by a fine not exceeding one hundred million won".[91]

Even if the pre-trades reporting is conducted at the time of the initial transaction, the legal mandate is not terminated. Post-trades reports must be made regularly or at any time when a change in terms of contract occurs. Consider a hypothetical case of a resident who intends to undertake overseas direct investment. In order to engage in FDI, he or she must report transaction details to a foreign exchange bank in advance, and report any subsequent changes in terms and conditions (e.g., extension of loan maturity, repayment methods, interest rates).[92] Also, regular reporting financial conditions (including invest-

The term "goods" here refers to movables, excluding means of payment and securities prescribed by the FETA. Moreover, a person who "has already made a report pursuant to Article 16 and 18 of the FETA exports or imports means of payment, etc. according to details of such report" is exempt from an extra reporting duty (Article 31(1) of enforcement decree of the FETA).

91 In lieu of this, the government may impose administrative fines not exceeding one hundred million won when a person "pays or receives funds without filing a report under Article 16 or after filing a false report", or administrative fines not exceeding 50 million won when a person "intends to export or import any means of payment or securities without filing a report pursuant to Article 17 or after filing a false report". See Article 32 of the FETA.

92 The term FDI under the FETA refers to any transactions, acts or payments by residents for the following reason that (i) "transactions or acts performed to establish continuous economic relations with a legal entity incorporated under the Acts and subordinate statutes of a foreign country (including a legal entity in the process of its incorporation) by acquiring securities issued by such legal entity or lending money to such legal entity", and "disbursement of funds to establish, expand or operate business offices in a foreign country or to conduct overseas business activities". See Art. 3(1)18 of the FETA. Article 8(1) of enforcement decree of the FETA explains that establishing continuous economic relations means any transactions or acts, which fall under any of the following items:

(i) an investment in which stocks or investment equities acquired to take part in the management of a juristic person established under foreign statutes account for not less than 10% of the total number of stocks issued or the total amount of equity investment made by the relevant foreign juristic person, (ii) the ratio of investment is less than 10%, but when there is a dispatch of executive officers, conclusion of a purchase and sale contract for raw materials or products for a term of one year or more, conclusion of a contract for offering and introducing technology or conducting joint research and development, or conclusion of a contract for receiving an order of overseas construction and industrial plant construction, (iii) acquisition of additional stocks or investment equities of a foreign juristic person already invested, (iv) loans

ment schedule, change in the ownership status) must be done at defined time intervals.[93] If the party has breached this rule and the amount of violation of an obligation to report exceeds one billion won, he or she may be "punished by imprisonment with labour for not more than one year or by a fine not exceeding one hundred million won" (Art. 29 of the FETA and Art. 40 of enforcement decree of the Act).[94]

Second, too much complicated rules of procedure of the Korean FX law are condemned to producing too many law-breakers.[95] Most breach cases uncovered by the regulators have been reportedly related to the failure to fulfil obligations to report. Indeed, in 2018, breaches of the pre-trades reporting duty, which was mainly caused by negligence, not malice, accounted for more than three-quarters of violations of the law (see Table 9).

Of course, some of the offenders could have shirked their reporting duties with the intention to move property abroad unknown to the authorities, or conceal the illicit origin and ownership of the proceeds of their unlawful activities. However, as Table 10 below displays, the government statistics confirm that a much larger proportion of breaches of the FX law are related to false reports made or omission, rather than to egregious activities such as money laundering.

Third, one of the drawbacks of too much detailed prescriptive approach to the regulation is that it could make market participants lose sight of the

---

with a maturity of not less than one year made to a relevant foreign juristic person by a resident who has invested therein.

93 The change in ownership status (ratio of shareholding) was previously subject to a pre-trades report. However, it has been converted to a post-trades report (within three months of the date of the event) since January 2018 (Art. 9–5(2) of the FETR), due to the reason that the rule is so tight that there is too much happening of the violations of the law.

94 The government may also impose administrative fines (the larger of 2% of the amount of violation or one million won), or issue a warning (when the amount of violation is less than $20,000 dollars), and suspend the transaction when there happen more than two times of violations in five years.

95 The FETA stipulates rules differently depending on the transaction amount. For example, in a case that a third party is involved in payment or receipt of a FX transaction, a (pre-trades) reporting is not required when the amount is less than $5,000 dollars, but it becomes mandatory when the transaction amount exceeds this level. Further, the relevant authorities that receive reports from the party to the transactions are different. That is, he or she must report to a foreign exchange bank if the amount ranges from $5,000 to $10,000, and to the Bank of Korea if the amount is larger than $10,000. Moreover, the threshold amount changes from time to time, making it difficult to grasp the exact application of the rules in practice.

TABLE 9 Violation cases of the FX law by types in 2018

Types	Direct investment	Real estate	Borrowing/ lending	Securities trades	Others	Total
Pre-trades Reporting (New item)	327	143	65	62	129	726 (56.7%)
Pre-trades Reporting (Changed item)	178	2038	65	1	13	277 (21.7%)
Post-trades reporting	200		–	–	2	240 (18.8%)
Payment/ receipt	–		–	–	29	29 (2.3%)
Registration	–		–	–	7	7 (0.5%)
Total	705	201	130	63	180	1,279 (100%)

SOURCE: FSS (2019)

TABLE 10 Detection records by types of breach

Types of breach	2015	2016	2017	2018	2019
Report an error or omission	44,456 (94.3%)	38,400 (93.4%)	38,285 (95.6%)	27,858 (91.4%)	31,832 (92.4%)
Flight of property	1,764 (3.7%)	2,198 (5.3%)	1,081 (2.7%)	2,508 (8.2%)	1,707 (4.9%)
Anti-money laundering	921 (2.0%)	529 (1.3%)	675 (1.7%)	112 (0.4%)	922 (2.7%)
Total	47,141 (100%)	41,127 (100%)	40,041 (100%)	30,478 (100%)	34,461 (100%)

SOURCE: CUSTOMS SERVICE DB

nature and purpose of the legal system. In particular, the highly complex set of rules (especially with respect to reporting) that enumerates the list of "do" or "do not" in every possible case may encourage the *box ticketing* of a party to the transactions: that is, the party may mistakenly assume that they only have to abide by rules that are explicitly engraved in the law without caring about any other social norms.[96] This is equivalent to saying that he or she tends to comply with the rules simply to avoid punishment, while disregarding the philosophy or *rechtsgut* (legal protection) of the regulation.

4.1.2 Issue Analysis

Despite the fact that most of permit or approval system have been eased to reporting or registration system under the new FETA regime, the Korean FX law has suffered criticism that the very tight pre-trades reporting rules restrict active transactions of individuals and corporations.[97]

A report (or reporting as a juristic act) is generally defined as "an official or formal statement of facts that have an influence on the legal status of a particular act, or to make it legally in force".[98] In theory, a report brings into its legal effect once the government has received the notification, but in practice, it can make a difference whether the authority will accept it or not.[99] In other words, the government may perform a due diligence when necessary, and refuse to accept it or recommend to modify the conditions of the transaction at issue. A natural question that then arises would be, "what is the difference between a report system that requires the authority's acceptance to initiate or proceed with transactions and a permit system that mandates the government's authorisation?" Admittedly, a transaction that requires a permit is deemed to be prohibitive in nature, whilst a transaction that has prerequisites of a report coupled with the relevant authority's acceptance is considered to less proscriptive, relying more upon the government's discretion. However, it is true that there is a blur, in reality, making it difficult to distinguish them.

This problem is more pronounced when we actually examine the languages of the FETA. The Korean FX law provides that a resident's acquisition of real

96 Goodhart et al. (1998), pp 2–3.

97 Indeed, the foreign exchange transactions regulation (FETR), which is promulgated by the finance minister pursuant to the FETA, consists of ten chapters, of which six chapters are devoted to stipulating the rules for reporting and the exceptions in detail.

98 Kim (2010), pp 113–117.

99 Article 40 of the Administrative Procedures Act provides that the "reporting obligation shall be deemed fulfilled upon the arrival of the report at the receiving agency", unless errors or omission are found in the report.

property abroad and a financial institution's overseas direct investment require *a priori* report with the government's acceptance; other capital transactions are, at least according to the legal text, not subject to the authority's review and acceptance once its report has been made. However, unfortunately, the reality is different. Above all, the reporting process is not completed only by one party's notification. A report (with the relevant supporting evidence) is destined to be checked by the government or a foreign exchange agency that has received the submission, and a party to the transaction cannot proceed with the subsequent procedure unless he or she obtains a written certificate from the authorities. For this reason, if it is an urgent deal, the party may miss a valuable investment opportunity.

In fact, it is questionable whether the main purpose of such a tight pre-trades reporting system is, as the government argues, to monitor the trends of foreign exchange transactions and to produce accurate data. Today, the Korean FX authorities are actively using a large volume of data collected and reported in quasi-real time through the Bank of Korea's Foreign Exchange Information System (FEIS) to identify trends in capital flows and to compile statistics.[100] Figure 5 below exhibits the work process of the system. As shown in this chart, when a foreign exchange agency enters every transactional data on the computer network system-connected to the FEIS, the Bank of Korea (international department) checks the accuracy of the data and confirms it. Further, reports created by the BOK staffs on the basis of it are provided to information users such as the Ministry of Economy and Finance (MOEF), regulatory agencies (Financial Services Commission, Financial Supervisory Service), and tax authorities (National Tax Service, Customs Service).

If monitoring or statistical matters are of main concern, operating the pre-trades reporting system as such is less convincing since the FX authorities are already able to effectively address these issues. Actually, owing to having this system, Korea is considered a rare case that can conduct a total inspection of FX transactions. As such, errors and omissions in the balance of payments (BOP) statistics of Korea are remarkably low compared to many other countries (see Figure 6).[101]

100 The FEIS was developed in April 1999, rightly after the Asian financial crisis, in order to collect and utilise every possible FX trading information in an instant and precise manner. This is the Korea's unique foreign exchange regulatory system, which is not found in the rest of the world.

101 According to the IMF, net errors and omissions in the BOP statistics in 2017 was reported as follows: China ($221.9 billion), United States ($92.2 billion), Japan ($35.8 billion),

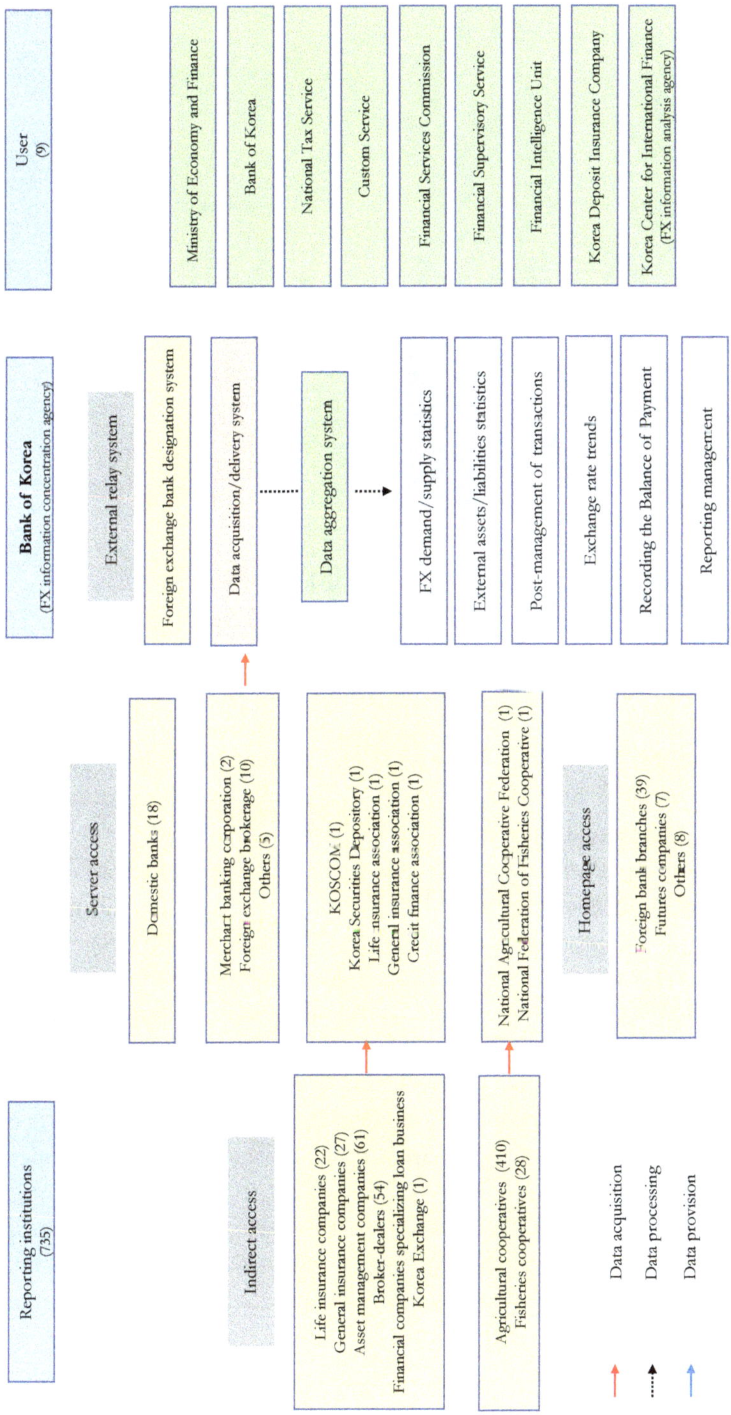

FIGURE 5 A workflow chart of the Foreign Exchange Information System (FEIS)
SOURCE: BOK (2013)

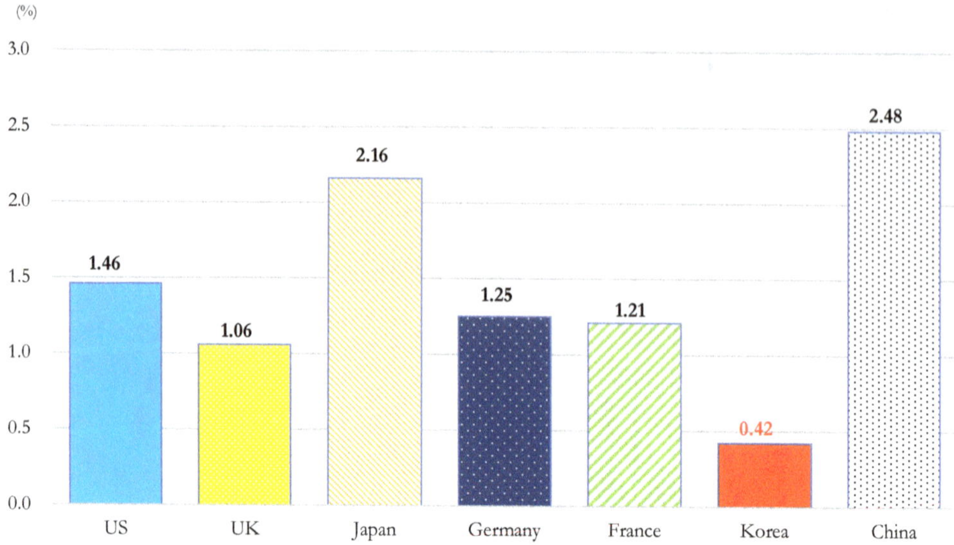

FIGURE 6 Net errors and omissions in the Balance of Payment: An international comparison
Note: Numbers (%) are calculated by dividing net errors and omissions in BOP by the sum of exports and imports for the period from 2008 to 2017.
SOURCE: IMF BALANCE OF PAYMENTS STATISTICS (BOPS); IMF BOP MANUAL

Against this backdrop, there has been a growing interest in replacing such a burdensome pre-trades reporting system with the post-trades reporting system. The post-trades reporting system is clearly advantageous in terms of enhancing autonomy of private transactions, and aforementioned problems of the pre-trades reporting system can be resolved in one fell swoop. However, admittedly, there is one drawback to this reform: the government's delayed recognition on the occurrence of transactions (or the conclusion of contracts) may retard policy response in an emergency. For this reason, in spite of numerous disadvantages, the Korean government has been reluctant to change the pre-trades reporting system from its roots. The FX authority has instead opted to alter the problematic provisions on an ad hoc basis, which has undermined the reputation of the Korean FX law, rendering the legal system a hodgepodge of confusing and complicated rules.

If so, a possible and reasonable solution to this problem would be to repeal the pre-trades reporting system and replace with post-trades reporting system, with the exception of special cases that the government has a good reason to

France ($22.1 billion), Germany ($19.7 billion), United Kingdom ($19.4 billion), and Korea ($8.7 billion).

figure out the nature of a contract in advance to prevent future crisis. A typical example is a resident's large volume of foreign currency borrowing. Given that the depth and liquidity of a FX market is yet low relative to developed markets, the rush of capital flows in a specific time can have a significant effect on the domestic market and its currency value.[102] This is why the Korean government currently mandates the pre-trades reporting to the MOEF prior to engaging in a foreign borrowing contract whose amount exceeds $30 million (including cumulative borrowings over the last year).[103] Similarly, a non-resident issuance of securities denominated in domestic currency is also subject to the pre-trades reporting obligations to the finance minister. This is, of course, because of the concern with the speculative attacks on Korean won.[104]

Taken together, it would be desirable to keep maintaining some of these pre-trades reporting rules until substantial further progress will be made toward a comparable level of the market depth and liquidity in the Korean FX market. Nevertheless, allowing such exceptions should be limited to the minimum necessary extent. Otherwise, the Korean FX law reform will end up failing in vain.

4.2 *Operation of the Legal System Relying Heavily upon Delegated Legislation*

4.2.1 Identifying the Key Issues

Much of the criticism surrounding the Korean FX law pertains to the issue of the supremacy of law. As already mentioned, most provisions in the FETA (a statute) have been written in such broad language that any person who wants to grasp the meaning of them has no choice but to consult with the FETR (an administrative rules).[105] Thus, it is even said that many practitioners

102 The Korean FX market is fast growing, but still has a long way to go compared to those of advanced countries, with a daily volume of $55 billion, merely accounting for 0.7% of total turnover in the world market. See BIS, *supra* n. 16.

103 Article 7–14 of the FETR. In doing so, the government intends to coordinate the schedule of borrowing contracts of large corporations in a scattered way, not on a specific date.

104 This is what we actually witnessed during the 1997 Asian finance crisis, when several currencies, including Thai baht and Indonesian rupiah, went under serious speculative attacks. In those times, many speculators (such as hedge funds) made huge profits by borrowing to sell the overvalued emerging market currencies massively with an expectation of the US dollar appreciation, and then paying back the borrowed currencies with less dollars when the dollar appreciation (or emerging market currencies' depreciation) is realised.

105 Actually, the provisions as to reporting obligations, which currently account for the largest proportion of the legal system, are largely written as follows: engraving in the FETA that "any person shall report ... when deemed necessary ... as prescribed by the presidential

(including regulators) do not seriously examine the law, but commonly resort to the administrative rules when reviewing specific issues.[106]

This way of handling the issues certainly causes a critical problem of undermining the principle of the *supremacy of the law* (or rule of law) that guarantees the democratic legitimacy of the legal system. Leaving the substantial authority to an administrative regulation, not a statute, furthermore, is prone to risk that comprehensive delegated legislation would be prevalent. That is, violating the principle of non-blanket delegation, the government executive could be tempted to rely more on its own rules and regulations than on a statute legislators make when it must discipline the market. It is always much easier and so convenient to circumvent the arduous legislative process. However, it should be noted that comprehensive delegated legislation always entails the problem of discretionary or abusive administrative power, rendering the legislative power to investigate and supervise the law-implementing activities of the government impotent. In particular, this can be more problematic in that violations of the rules, in some cases, result in severe criminal punishments.[107]

Another problem of a heavy reliance upon delegated legislation is that such an approach may lead to confusion and even conflict in interpretation or application of the law. In actuality, we encounter not a few cases in which the FETA (a statute) lacks clarity in the definition of terms, and new concepts emerge in sub-decree or administrative rules. Accordingly, practitioners often set their own criteria on interpretating the legal provisions, disregarding the language in text. The following are some relevant examples.

First, the concept of the *residency* (i.e., distinguishing the difference between a resident and a non-resident) is not clearly defined in the FETA,

---

decree", and subsequently in its enforcement decree that "for more details ... as publicly notified by the finance minister". For example, Article 18(1) of the FETA provides that "any person who intends to perform capital transactions, shall file a report on such capital transactions with the Minister of Economy and Finance pursuant to Presidential Decree", and Article 32(1) of its enforcement decree in turn provides that "any person who intends to file a report on capital transactions pursuant to Article 18(1) of the Act shall submit to the Minister of Economy and Finance the documents for reporting determined and publicly notified by the Minister of Economy and Finance. In such cases, detailed matters concerning reporting procedures, methods, etc. of report shall be determined and publicly notified by the Minister of Economy and Finance". And then, the FETR provides details in three chapters, ranging from 7 to 9.

106 Kim (2015), p 251.

107 To be sure, the FETA only presents punishments provisions without much explanation, and almost all elements that constitute a crime are prescribed in the FETR determined by the finance minister.

causing trouble for application of the law in practice.[108] Subparagraph 14 of Article 3(1) of the FETA defines a resident as "an individual who has a domicile or residence in Korea, and a legal entity whose main office is located in Korea"; and subgraph 15 of the same provision defines a non-resident as "an individual and a legal entity other than residents".[109] However, unfortunately, this simple definition provides little information for determining the residency. For instance, according to this provision, any person whose main source of income is in a foreign country may be also deemed a resident as long as he or she has an abode in Korea. This way of thinking is nevertheless inconsistent with the court's reasoning. The Supreme Court once held that "admittedly, there might be cases wherein the distinction of the residency is not clear when a person has a residence both in Korea and in other foreign countries; in such case, further consideration needs to be given to the immigration records or the duration (actual length) of stay".[110] Moreover, the Constitutional Court ruled that "a residency is basically irrelevant of a nationality, and it is rather centred on the idea that he or she has lived for a certain period of time with his or her substantial economic interest".[111]

For this reason, more specific criteria are established in the sub-decree. As shown in Table 11, Article 10 of the enforcement decree of the Act lists the detailed instances wherein a person is classified as a resident or a non-resident for each situation he or she faces. But nor could be this a complete solution, because it is nearly impossible to describe all possible situations with some words. That is, even if referring to the provision of the enforcement decree, there could be a number of cases in which the authority is not sure of determining the residency. For instance, in the case of a person with dual nationality (or dual citizenship), it may be ambiguous whether he or she should be regarded

108 Identifying the residency of a party to the transaction is a crucial part of application of the law, since the FETA deals with a resident differently than a non-resident when invoking the rules.

109 Nevertheless, "branch offices, local offices or other offices of non-residents located in Korea, shall be deemed residents regardless of whether such offices, etc. have legal authority to act as an agent thereof" (Article 3(1)15 of the FETA).

110 Supreme Court Decision 99 Do362 Decided 9 April 1999.

111 Constitutional Court en banc Decision 2003Hun-Ba114 Decided 30 June 2005. Having said that, a nationality (a legal identification of a person as a subject of a sovereign state) seems to be also an important element when determining his or her residency. For example, a Korean national is legally classified to be a non-resident when he or she resides more than two years abroad, but the legal status is changed to a resident only three months after returning home. On the other hand, a foreign national becomes a resident when he or she resides more than six months in Korea. As such, the FETA maintains the policy stance of recognising a Korean national as a resident as broad as possible.

as a non-resident or a resident one year after leaving the country: if the government has assumed that the person is a foreign national, he or she would be classified as a non-resident, because three months have already passed. Conversely, if the authority has assumed that the person is a Korean national, he or she would be classified as a resident, because two years have not yet passed.[112] There also occurred a split of the Supreme Court's decisions on the issue regarding the relationship between a foreign subsidiary (or branch) and a head office in Korea. On one hand, the highest court held that "foreign currency transactions between a paper company established by a resident in a tax haven and a foreign corporation are presumed to be transactions between a resident and a non-resident, not transactions between non-residents".[113] On the other hand, the Court ruled in another case that "in connection with the establishment of a foreign sub-subsidiary, the head office (parent company) was not found guilty of failing to report changes in overseas direct investment, because there was a sufficient economic reason for the acquisition of shares of stock of sub-subsidiary by the subsidiary".[114] That is, the Supreme Court thought that the transaction occurred between non-residents.

In this respect, it becomes clear that we had better focus on the economic substance of the transaction in question and the subject of the transaction in determining the residency. This way of thinking is consistent with the decision of the Constitutional Court referred above. Lawmakers should consider this when revising the law in the future.

Second, there are some cases wherein a completely new concept is introduced in the administrative rules, not in the law. A typical or good example of this is the "currency-linked foreign securities whose value is tied to Korean won".[115] As previously mentioned, a transaction of assets denominated or paid

112 With the amendment of the Nationality Act in January 2011, dual nationality (or dual citizenship) is, albeit to a limited extent, was permitted.

113 Supreme Court Decision 2006 Do7881 Decided 15 February 2008; Supreme Court Decision 2006 Du7904 Decided 12 March 2009.

114 Supreme Court Decision 2015Do5312 Decided 15 June 2017. In this ruling, the Court asserted that "an overseas subsidiary's establishment of another local subsidiary by acquiring shares of a foreign corporation is not considered as overseas direct investment wherein a resident is subject to reporting obligations under Article 18 (1) of the FETA, because the party to the transaction (i.e., overseas subsidiary) deems a non-resident. However, a resident should fulfil the reporting duty when he or she has acquired the stock for his or her own economic interest, or when an overseas subsidiary is a company that exists only on paper".

115 The term "currency-linked foreign securities whose value is tied to Korean won" literally means foreign securities whose payment value is determined or settled by the Korean won (see subparagraph 23 of Article 1–2 of the FETR).

TABLE 11 Criterion for determining the residency (Article 10 of enforcement decree of the FETA)

Classification		Residents	Non-residents
Individuals	Korean nationals	– Persons dispatched to and stay in a foreign country for the purpose of working for an overseas diplomatic mission of Korea – Persons staying in Korea for more than three months after entering Korea as a non-resident – Other persons need to be recognised as a resident considering the conditions of business, primary place of stay, etc., and are determined by the finance minister	– Persons engaging in business activities in a foreign country – Persons serving in international organisations in a foreign country – Persons staying in a foreign country for not less than two years. In case of temporary stay in Korea for not more than three months, the period of stay shall be deemed to be included in the said two-year period – Other persons need to be recognised as non-residents considering the conditions of business, primary place of stay, etc., and are determined by the finance minister
	Foreigners	– Persons engaging in business activities in the Republic of Korea – Persons staying in Korea for not less than six months	– Diplomats serving in foreign missions or international organisations in Korea and their attendants or employees – Persons entering Korea to perform public duties for foreign governments or international organisations – Persons staying in a foreign country for more than three months after leaving Korea as resident foreigners

TABLE 11 Criterion for determining the residency (Article 10 of enforcement decree of the FETA) (*cont.*)

Classification	Residents	Non-residents
Corporates, entity, etc.	– Overseas diplomatic missions of Korea – Organisations, agencies or other equivalent entities whose main offices are in Korea	– Diplomatic missions of foreign governments and international organisations in Korea – The US Armed Forces and UN Forces equivalent thereto in accordance with the Agreement under Article IV of the Mutual Defence Treaty between Korea and the US, regarding Facilities and Areas and the Status of US Armed Forces in Korea, members, civilian military employees, invited contractors thereof, and non-appropriated fund agencies, military post offices and military banks of the US Armed Forces, etc. – Business offices or other offices of a domestic juristic person, etc. in a foreign country – Organisations, agencies or other equivalent entities whose main offices are in a foreign country

Note: Family members living together and mainly dependent upon a resident or non-resident for their living shall be classified as residents or non-residents, according to the classification of such residents or non-residents.

in a foreign currency between non-residents in a foreign country is not a regulated activity under the FETA (see Article 2 of the Act). However, if the value of the securities varies with the value of the domestic currency, to put it another way, if the securities is issued as currency-linked foreign securities whose value is tied to Korean won, the party to the transaction (in this case, a non-resident) must report details of the issuance to the Ministry of Economy and Finance (or the Korean finance minister) in advance.[116]

It is not desirable to define any new material term in the administrative rules, not specifying it in the underlying law, because it may lead to many controversial issues in interpreting the relevant provisions. Definitely, it will hinder a stable and predictable legal system. Lawmakers should consider this when revising the law in the future.

Third, the Korean FX law endorses the "territorial principle" that is in application to foreign exchange transactions in Korea, "personal principle" that is in application to a resident's foreign exchange transactions, and "protectionism" that is in application to foreign exchange transactions related to the national interests of Korea.[117] As such, the law is so comprehensive in scope that law enforcers often have a difficulty in applying the law provision to a particular case. Above all, a lack of clarity of the language of Article 2 of the FETA caused even the authorities to develop their own criteria for invoking the Act, disregarding the legal text. That is, in actual practice, the Korean government simplifies the covered person and activities as follows: (i) transactions of assets denominated (or settled) in foreign currency between residents, (ii) transactions of assets between a resident and a non-resident, (iii) transactions of assets denominated (or settled) in domestic currency between non-residents (see Table 12).

TABLE 12 Objects of application of the FETA

Counterparties	Currencies (denomination/settlement)	Application of the law (Yes or No)
Resident ↔ Resident	Korean won	No
Resident ↔ Resident	Foreign currency	Yes
Resident ↔ Non-resident	Korean won, Foreign currency	Yes
Non-resident ↔ Non-resident	Korean won	Yes
Non-resident ↔ Non-resident	Foreign currency	No

SOURCE: BOK (2018)

116 Article 7–23(1)2 of the FETR.

117 BOK (2016), p 18.

However, this short-cut method is not without its problem. As in the case of currency-linked foreign securities referred above or a Kimchi bond (a foreign currency-denominated bond issued in the Korean market.), a non-resident may be obliged to fulfil his or her obligation to report transactional details to the authorities, even if the counterparty is a non-resident. Therefore, to be exact, every foreign exchange transaction is covered under the FETA, with the exception of a transaction of assets in Korean won between residents in Korea and a transaction of assets in foreign currency between non-residents overseas.

4.2.2 Issue Analysis

In a democratic system based on the principle of separation of powers and the rule of law (or supremacy of law), essential matters concerning the freedom and rights of the people may be restricted only by laws enacted by legislators who are the representatives of the people. However, it is also true that more prompt as well as flexible legislative actions are required in the modern society that is increasingly sophisticated and changing faster. Given that the legislative capacity of lawmakers is limited in terms of expertise and timeliness, legislators hereby delegate some of their authorities to other state institution, *inter alia*, the government executive, and allow it to govern the people. In fact, it is not technically possible to establish all detailed rules and regulations by law.

There is one caveat though, that delegated (also known as subordinate) legislation should not be always and everywhere allowed. Notwithstanding the foregoing justification, excessive expansion of the delegation may threaten the overarching principles (i.e., separation of power, rule of law) of a constitutional democracy, which would seriously undermine a national legal order. It is right for legislators endowed with a democratic legitimacy and authority in law-making to make a critical decision, and a heavy reliance on the government's discretion would likely distort the outcome, because government officials are more susceptible to the lobbying of interest-advocacy groups.[118] Therefore, delegated legislation must come with a control device correspondingly, and the Korean legislative system has adopted the "principle of statutory reservation" and the "non-blanket-delegation doctrine" to this end.

118 Lowi (1987), pp 302–303. See also Constitutional Court Decision 2001Hun-Ma882 Decided 25 March 2004. In this ruling, the Court held that "the legislative process of the National Assembly (the Korean parliament) is to make important decisions, reflecting the people's opinions through free and open discussion (or debate). This is a more democratic process in the sense that lawmakers usually accept criticism of the general public or the opposing party in order to coordinate the conflicting interests, as opposed to administrative rule-making procedures by a limited number of government officials".

The principle of statutory reservation indicates that every administrative action must be based on a statute law. However, it should be noted that "it nonetheless requires legislators to make their own decisions on critical matters regarding the fundamental rights of the people".[119] Furthermore, even if there is an underlying law, courts will find it illegal when it establishes new requirements or standards in the stage of specifying delegated rules.[120]

Moreover, the non-blanket-delegation doctrine indicates that delegation must be done in a clear and specific manner, not in an obscure and comprehensive manner. Article 75 of the Constitution Act makes it clear that "the president may issue presidential decrees concerning matters delegated to him or her by Act with the scope specifically defined and also matters necessary to enforce Acts". With respect to this provision, the Constitutional Court interprets that "the law must determine the essential element and scope to be stipulated in administrative rules, so that any person may draw a contour map of the regulations".[121]

The Court presents the following criteria that are used when reviewing the constitutionality of cases. First, it considers the extent of the infringement of fundamental rights. Specifically, it demands a higher standard for clarity and concreteness of delegation, when the freedom and rights of the people are deemed to be restricted with high probability. Relatedly, in the case of penalty (or punishment) provisions, the scope of delegation and its requirements are bound to be limited.[122] Second, when the regulatory environments keep changing, or when covered persons are not general public but the professional experts in their fields, the requirement for clarity of delegation might be eased.[123] Third, if the regulatory impact is significant, or a national security is at stake, the aim, scope, and means of regulations should be specified in the law. Fourth and last, procedural legitimacy is also a factor for consideration. The Court herein looks at the role of public participation, due diligence, and other legitimacy-related concerns when making statutory instruments.

In light of these considerations, there seems to be a serious flaw in the Korean FX law and regulatory system. Above all else, the fact that a host of administrative rules are promulgated by the finance minister as a form of public notice raises a concern over legitimacy in both substantive and procedural

119 Constitutional Court Decision 98Hun-Ba70 Decided 27 May 1999.

120 Supreme Court Decision 2009Du17797 Decided 29 April 2010.

121 Constitutional Court Decision 2005Hun-Ma161, 189 (merged) Decided 27 November 2008.

122 Due to the principle of *nulla poena sine lege* (no penalty without a law), delegating the authority of provisioning (criminal) punishment to sub-regulations is generally not allowed (Constitutional Court en banc Decision 2007Hun-Ma949 Decided 24 September 2009).

123 Constitutional Court en banc Decision 90Hun-Ga27 Decided 11 February 1991.

perspectives. Of course, the Framework Act on Administrative Regulations accommodates the government's practice, stipulating that "when the statutes or regulations mandate professional, technical or minor matters which need to be mandated due to relevant extenuating circumstances considering the nature of affairs by specifying the scope thereof in detail, regulations may be prescribed by public notice".[124] Also, the courts even recognise that "administrative rules per se that have no legal effects may become the (legally binding) statutory instruments in combination with higher statutes or regulations."[125] It should be noted, however, that such lax standards in favour of delegated legislation would likely lead to abuse of the government's power.[126] On a related note, the Supreme Court argued that "administrative rules only have legal effects to the extent that they have the function of supplementing the provisions of the higher statute law, and even if a public notice (as an administrative rule) is based on a law, the legal effect will be lost when the delegated rule creates a new dimension of regulation beyond what the higher statute delegates to it".[127] In this regard, a host of reporting provisions that are largely written in the FETR (a public notice), not the FETA (a statute) seem to lack legitimacy in terms of the principle of legal certainty. Particularly, comprehensive delegation in this area should be avoided, because a breach of reporting rules may result in severe administrative or criminal sanctions, frequently raising the issues of infringement of fundamental rights.

In addition, attention needs to be paid to the fact that the rule-making or revision process of administrative rules (in this case, a public notice) is not so strict. For example, Article 25 of the Regulations on Management of Legislative Affairs just provides that "the head of each central administrative agency may request the Ministry of Government Legislation to examine and review public notices (including regulations, rules, instructions, guidelines, notification, etc. issued in direct connection with the enforcement of statutes) to ensure its legitimacy", and does not require any formal procedures comparable to the enactment of law. Moreover, the National Assembly Act mandates that the competent standing committee examines whether the presidential decree and the ordinance of the prime minister or each minister are not in conformed with the purpose or contents of the higher statute, and take necessary

124 Art. 4(2) of the Framework Act on Administrative Regulations.

125 Constitutional Court Decision 99Hun-Ba91 Decided 28 October 2004. See also the Supreme Court Decision 86Nu484 Decided 29 September 1987.

126 If the government officials make a bill that delegates the authority to stipulate critical rules to them, and legislators merely pass the bill, the legislative power will be effectively transferred to the executive branch. See Lee (2007), p 65.

127 Supreme Court Decision 97Nu13474 Decided 26 November 1999.

actions for correcting them, such as "submitting to the speaker (or chairperson) a report on the result of the examination, including the progress of the examination and opinion on the handling thereof" or "notifying the head of the competent central administrative agency of the details thereof". However, there is no such control device in the case of a public notice. Similarly, while Article 13–2 of the Act on the Promulgation of Statutes stipulates that "statutes, presidential decrees, ordinances of the prime minister, and ordinances of ministries directly related to the limitation of rights or the imposition of obligations on people shall enter into force at least 30 days after the date of their promulgation, except in cases where special grounds for urgent enforcement exist", Article 6 of the Regulations on the Promotion of Administrative Efficiency and Collaboration provides that a public notice "shall take effect (only) 5 days after the date of their promulgation, except in cases where the effective date is specified".

Taken together, it would be desirable to engrave every single critical provision in the FETA. With respect to procedural regulations including so many existing reporting rules, nevertheless, we also know all too well that it is nearly impossible to describe all the contents in the law. In fact, this problem would not be resolved unless there is a complete overhaul of reporting system. Before long, the Korean legislature will be confronted with this issue.

4.3 *Operation of the Bank-Oriented Legal System*

4.3.1 Identifying the Key Issues

One of the features that characterise the Korean FX system is the "foreign exchange bank system", which indicates that "every foreign exchange transaction must be carried out via the authorised banks that are registered with the finance minister".[128] Under this system, banks deal with regulatory affairs such as receiving reports and confirming the legality of customers' transactions on behalf of the government, and the FX authorities can catch the trends in capital flows through the banks.

The reason why the Korean government has adopted such a system is quite straightforward. This is a very convenient and efficient system to monitor cross-border transactions and to manage the records as far as the FX authority is concerned. For example, banks deal with most of the pre-trades reporting affairs and post-trades management, and the government simply has to

128 The foreign exchange bank system has to date formed the basis of the Korean FX regulatory framework since its inception with the enactment of the FECA (Act no. 933, in December 1961). See MOEF, *supra* n. 63.

regulate and supervise the banks.[129] This system also benefits the banks, since they are allowed to operate every kind of FX businesses defined in the FETA in exchange for that, enjoying a privileged status in the market. In particular, some businesses such as international payments and receipts, receipt of foreign currency deposits may be run only by the banks.[130]

However, there is a growing consensus that there is only so much this system properly works toward achieving the policy objectives of the FX law in today's rapidly changing financial environment. Although the needs to promote the FX and capital markets for the purpose of enhancing the market depth and liquidity are higher than ever, it seems that the bank-oriented legal system has not been so successful in encouraging more diverse players to take active part in the markets. Indeed, until recently, the FX business regulation of the financial institutions has been operated in favour of the banking industry. As previously mentioned, the registered banks may engage in any FX transactions. However, other financial institutions (such as securities firms, insurance companies, etc.) as opposed to banks were only able to run the businesses that the FETR permits them to operate. The administrative rules enumerated the list of services that can be provided by each industry (i.e., positive regulation). As a result, the legal system received a large amount of criticism that it was the main cause of undermining the competitiveness of the overall domestic financial markets and industries. On 22 March 2016, the Korean government hereby switched it to the quasi-negative regulation, amending the relevant provisions in the FETR. That is, each industry player has been allowed to freely enter the FX market and do the business to the extent that the law and regulations do not explicitly prohibit it (see Table 13). For instance, a broker-dealer today can operate any FX businesses other than core banking services, including international payments and receipts, receipt of foreign currency deposits.

It would be probably premature to evaluate changes in the system and to draw any conclusion of it. However, the Korean government seems to believe that competition in the FX market is still insufficient and that consumer welfare has not been yet increased to a satisfactory level following an amendment of the rules.[131] For example, in the case of small-amount overseas remittance business, according to the authority, "competition is being hampered by the formidable structure of bank-oriented business," despite the implementation

---

129 Banks are reportedly to process more than 95% of all foreign exchange transaction reports. See Kang (2017), p 83.

130 These are also defined as banking services within the scope of the Banking Act (Article 27).

131 MOEF (2018).

TABLE 13 Scope of FX businesses available to each financial sector

	Governing law	Before (Do)	After (Do not)
Bank	Banking Act, etc.	All affairs	–
Postal services	Act on Special Cases Concerning the Management of Postal Services	Money exchanges, Money order purchase	
Merchant bank	Financial Investment Services and Capital Markets Act	All affairs excluding deposit taking	Deposit taking
Securities firm/ Trust company		Money exchanges for securities/derivatives trade	Payments/receipts, Deposit taking
Korea Securities Finance Corp.		–	
Insurance company	Insurance Business Act	Insurance contract, Loan	
Savings bank/ Credit union	Mutual Savings Banks Act/Credit Unions Act	Money exchanges	Payments/receipts, Borrowing and lending
MG community credit cooperative	Community Credit Cooperatives Act	–	
Financial company specialising in loan business	Specialised Credit Finance Business Act	Loan, Facility rental	Payments/receipts, Deposit taking
Payment gateway	Electronic Financial Transactions Act	Current transactions settlement	Payments/receipts, Deposit taking, Securities (means of international payment) issuance and trade

Note: After revisions to the FETR, it is possible to operate FX businesses directly related to the core business of each financial institution.
SOURCE: MOEF (2016A)

of market entry deregulation for non-financial tech companies, thereby failing to expand consumer choice.[132]

Against this backdrop, the Korean government has decided to further ease the regulation, with a special focus on broadening the scope of non-bank financial institutions (i.e., other foreign exchange agencies). According to the government's plan set forth in September 2018, the authority has allowed non-bank financial institutions such as securities firms, credit card companies to engage in money exchange and transfer (or remittance) business, albeit a small amount.[133] Also, it permitted the "comprehensive financial investment business entities" with equity capital of more than 4 trillion won to issue the foreign currency denominated commercial papers.[134] These are truly significant changes to the regulatory regime in that the legal system has started to allow non-bank institutions to operate some of core business of banks. Today, the Korean government is contemplating further deregulating the FX market and industry, and in doing so, it intends not only to promote competition, including the market entry of new competitors, but also to improve competitiveness of the domestic financial system as a whole.

4.3.2 Issue Analysis

Banks are most definitely important foreign exchange agencies given the nature and the scope of their businesses. Indeed, a glance at the definition of the terms stipulated in the law tells us that banks are classified as "the foreign exchange agencies", whereas non-bank financial institutions are classified as "other foreign exchange agencies".[135] However, the recent financial

132 Ibid. When sending money to a bank account overseas, the burden of fees that consumers bear is high due to the monopoly power of banks in the business. In case overseas remittances are made through banks, consumers pay 4~5% of the amount as a fee.

133 As of 1 January 2019, the limit was initially set to be $3,000 per item and $30,000 per year, but four months later, on 3 May of the same year, the limit was increased to $5,000 per item and $50,000 per year. In addition, savings banks with assets of more than 1 trillion won were allowed to provide money transfer services up to $5,000 per item and $50,000 per year, and the remittance limit for a specialised foreign exchange dealer was also raised up to $5,000 per item and $50,000 per year. See MOEF, *supra* n. 131.

134 Article 77–2 of the FISCMA stipulates that "the Financial Services Commission may designate as a comprehensive financial investment business entity an investment trader or investment broker who is (i) a stock company under the Commercial Act, (ii) who engages in business of underwriting securities, (iii) whose equity capital shall reach or exceed 3 trillion won, and (iv) who meets other criteria prescribed by enforcement decree taking into consideration the risk management ability, etc. of the relevant investment trader or investment broker in carrying out the credit offering service".

135 Art. 8(5) of the FETA, Art. 14 of its enforcement decree and Article 2–12 of the FETR.

environment has been fast-changing, threatening the current foreign exchange bank system. Above all, the scope of foreign exchange business of non-bank financial institutions continues to expand due to the government policies aiming at reinforcing resilience of the financial system by promoting the market depth and liquidity of foreign exchange. In addition, we observe that new FX products are continuously emerging in the market in the midst of rapid technological change especially in the field of payment and settlement.

It would be quite difficult to effectively respond to the radically-changed regulatory landscape with the existing legal system. Particularly concerning the "foreign exchange bank system", there is much criticism that the gap between law and practice is increasing. Below is a discussion of the issue that has been identified as a new challenge to the government, which tackles the problem surrounding the confirmation duty of foreign exchange banks defined in Article 10(1) of the FETA.

Article 10(1) of the FETA stipulates that "when a foreign exchange agency, a specialised foreign exchange dealer, and a foreign exchange brokerage company makes transactions subject hereto with their customers, it shall confirm whether transactions, payment or receipts of their customers are permitted or reported under this Act".[136] This provision has a great significance in the sense that the law dictates how foreign exchange banks can go about detecting and screening out suspicious FX transactions in the first round. For this reason, any staff members or employees who are in breach of confirmation duty while dealing with the customers' transactions at the foreign exchange banks can be seriously punished, including a prison sentence. That is, they may be subject to administrative disposition such as the "suspension of business for a period of two months" (Article 12(1) of the FETA and Article 22 (<annex 2>) of its enforcement decree), and may also be "punished by imprisonment with labour for not more than one year or by a fine not exceeding one hundred million won" (Article 29 of the FETA).[137]

136 This provision was originally Article 10 of the FETA (confirmation obligation in performing duties), but it was located in paragraph (1) with an amendment to the Act that has introduced a new provision of market abuse prohibitions (paragraph (2)). The foreign exchange bank system has played an important role in regulating FX transactions in Korea to date for nearly 60 years since its inception when the old FECA initially implemented it.

137 When a foreign exchange agency is suspended from its business for two months, the authority may also impose penalty surcharges not exceeding 40% of unjust enrichment on the institution (Article 12–2 of the FETA and Article 23 (<annex 3>) of its enforcement decree).

If so, is the law enforcement so stringent as the provisions written in the Act? The answer is "no, not really". It seems not to be treated all that seriously in banking practice, and in particular, it is very rare for an offender to be punished as stipulated in the law when being in violation of Article 10(1) of the FETA. Actually, according to the sanction records by the regulator, there have been no criminal accusations (or indictments), and most of the cases ended with administrative guidance or low-level dispositions, such as warning notices, action requests.[138] More specifically, a total of 18 offences alleged of a violation of Article 10(1) of the FETA were detected through the full investigation by the Financial Supervisory Service (FSS) over the past 6 years, of which 15 cases were merely closed with action requests.[139]

In fact, it should come as no surprise. Given that the persistent easing of entry rules for business erodes the dominant position of banking sector in the FX industry and competition in the market is getting fierce, it has become difficult for the government to impose extra regulatory burdens only on banks. The problem is that banks' weakened incentive to fulfil the obligations to confirm their customers' transactions diligently and carefully coupled with the authority's lenient law enforcement may put consumers using FX services at risk of violating the law. The Korean government hereby responds to this problem with administrative guidance, encouraging banks to provide their customers with clearer explanations on the pre-trades reporting obligations.[140] However, we believe that this only adds a further burden to bank employees in charge of customer reports, and thus cannot be a feasible solution. The FX authority should come up with a more fundamental solution without procrastination.

There is a big caveat to the conclusion, though: even if increasingly expanding the scope of FX businesses permitted to nonbank financial institutions is generally deemed to be an irreversible market trends, the role and systematic status of the FX regulation in the financial law system must also be considered. Adopting the principle of "same activity, same risk, same regulation" is recommended in this regard. That is, it would be reasonable and justifiable for regulators to further strengthen the FX related prudential requirements for

---

138 Action requests was introduced in January 2004 for the purpose of strengthening internal control system of financial institutions by notifying the heads of the companies of unlawful behaviours of their employees and mandating them to take appropriate disciplinary actions.

139 The remainder of 3 cases were closed with suspension of service (2) or reprimand (1). See Kang, *supra* n. 129, p 86.

140 See MOEF, *supra* n. 131.

nonbank foreign exchange business operators, as their entry into a new business may add on the extra risk to entire finance system.[141]

5 Proposals for Amendment of the Legal System

5.1 *A Complete Overhaul of the FX law*

Despite the fact that there has been much progress, the FETA still has a long way to go to achieve its policy objectives. This is because there still remain many control devices of the old FX law (or the FECA), hindering active transactions in FX market. Given the increased cross-border trades and the need for development of the domestic financial markets, however, the Korean FX law should be complete-overhauled. It has to be transformed into a legal system that fully serves a purpose of stabilising the foreign exchange market, reinforcing external soundness on the premise of enhanced market depth and revitalisation of the market function. In doing so, the FX law would contribute to robust development of the Korean financial markets as a whole.

5.1.1 Reframe the "Procedure-Oriented" System into the "Function-Oriented" System

It should be noted that a stopgap upon which the Korean government has relied up to date, that is, intermittently revising only the problematic parts of the administrative rules on ad hoc basis, has made the matter worse. Today, market participants face a hodgepodge of rules that are governing their transactions, which exposes them to much legal or regulatory risk. To be sure, this contradicts the legislative intent of the FETA that strives to ensure stability in the foreign exchange market by facilitating active currency transactions.

In this respect, it is required to abolish or simplify procedural measures, *inter alia*, reporting regulations, which account for a large part of the current legal system. As will be shown later, most reporting rules are better suited to anti-money laundering legislation that aims to detect and control illicit financial transactions. Legislators have to make the Korean FX law a special law that provides a legal basis for the government's exchange rate policy, FX related macroprudential regulations, and the currency market abuse prohibitions. Ergo, we propose that the structure of the FETA should be reframed as follows

141 As mentioned earlier, this is what the Korean government did on June 2016 when it started to ease FX business regulation, and accordingly imposed the macroprudential stability levy on nonbank financial institutions as well – prior to the rule amendment, the subject of this regulation had been limited to commercial banks.

(see Figure 7). In doing so, the Korean FX law that is notorious for a very strict procedural regulation shall be transformed into a rather flexible functional regulation. The reason why it is called "functional" lies in the fact that the regulatory system will be reframed in accordance with each policy goal under the purview of properly designed financial laws, with a special focus on regulating the underlying, and thus more fundamental, economic functions of foreign exchange transactions.[142]

First, Chapter 2 will provide the government's measures and means to stabilise the value of its currency (Korean won) and to secure external soundness. These include various macroprudential policy and capital control (or safeguard) measures, in addition to the market intervention tools. Also, the Foreign Exchange Equalisation Fund, which is presently a separate chapter, will be incorporated into a new Chapter 2. Such an amendment is reasonable, taking into account the fact that the purpose of establishing the Foreign Exchange Equalisation Fund is to raise funds for intervention in the foreign exchange market. Second, market abuse behaviours including currency rigging will be strictly prohibited under Chapter 3 (Foreign Exchange Business Regulation and Supervision). Third, as discussed infra, the current Chapter 4 that stipulates the procedures for transactions will be much simplified because most pre-trades reports are repealed and replaced with post-trades reports in a way that ease much regulatory burden on those who engage in FX transactions.[143]

Chapter	**Current Law**
1	General Provisions
2	Foreign Exchange Agencies, etc.
3	Foreign Exchange Equalisation Fund
4	Payments and Transactions
5	Supplementary Provisions
6	Penalty Provisions

Chapter	**Proposal for revision**
1	General Provisions
2	Market Intervention and Macroprudential FX Regulations
3	Foreign Exchange Business: Regulation and Supervision
4	Reporting and Inspections
5	Supplementary Provisions
6	Penalty Provisions

FIGURE 7 A proposal for amendment of the structure of Foreign Exchange Transactions Act

142 In this context, the "functional regulation" must be distinguished from a so-called "functional approach to financial supervision", which means that the purview of supervisory agencies is "based not on entities but on the business being transacted". See Schwarcz (2014).

143 If so, Article 10(1) of the FETA that stipulates the (pre-trades reports) confirmation duty of foreign exchange agencies. has no reason to be anymore, since those who conduct FX transactions will have only to comply with post-trades reporting obligations.

5.1.2 Clearly Define the Regulatory Scope

Criticism of the Korean FX law includes the arguments regarding the lack of clarity of the regulatory scope. The FETA is written in such a subtle and broad manner with respect to objects of application of the law. Further, in many cases, main contents of rules are entirely delegated to the subordinate executive orders (i.e., the FETR promulgated by the finance minister). As a consequence, the legal system has become complicated and convoluted to a degree that even lawyers specialising in FX affairs complain of difficulty interpreting the law.

TABLE 14 A proposal for an amendment of the FETA

Current law	Proposals for revisions
Article 2 (Objects of Application) (1) This Act shall apply to any of the following matters: 1. Foreign exchange in Korea, foreign exchange transactions conducted therein, or other acts related thereto 2. Transactions, payments or receipts between Korea and any foreign country, or other acts related thereto (including those which are performed in any foreign country and which have an effect in Korea) 3. Transactions between an individual having a domicile or residence in a foreign country and a legal entity having a main office in a foreign country, which are denominated or payable in the currency of Korea, or other acts related thereto 4. Acts conducted by an individual having a domicile or residence in Korea, or his/her agents, employers or other employees in connection with his/her assets or business in a foreign country 5. Acts conducted by a representative, agents, employers or other employees of a legal entity having its main office in Korea in connection with assets or business of the legal entity in a foreign country	**Article 2 (Objects of Application)** (1) This Act shall apply to *any matters other than the following*: 1. *Any transactions, payments or receipts of a domestic currency (Korean won) in Korea between residents, and other acts related thereto.* 2. *Any transactions, payments or receipts of a foreign currency abroad between non-residents, and other acts related thereto.*

TABLE 14 A proposal for an amendment of the FETA (*cont.*)

Current law	Proposals for revisions
Article 3 (Definitions) (1) The definitions of terms used in this Act shall be as follows: 8. The term "securities in foreign currency" means securities denominated in a foreign currency, or those payable in a foreign country 14. The term "resident" means an individual who has a domicile or residence in Korea, and a legal entity whose main office is located in Korea	**Article 3 (Definitions)** (1) The definitions of terms used in this Act shall be as follows: 8. The term "securities in foreign currency" means securities denominated in a foreign currency, or those payable in a foreign country (*including currency-linked foreign securities whose value is tied to Korean won*). 14. The term "resident" means an individual or a legal entity *who resides for a certain period of time, or engages in economic activities.*

Ergo, we propose that several provisions under the FETA that has suffered from uncertainty and ambiguity should be made clear as follows (see Table 14).

First, given that the language of Article 2 of this Act is not clear-cut, and practitioners (including the government officials) interpret the text in a simplified way that "all FX affairs other than any transactions, payments or receipts of Korean won in Korea between residents and any transactions, payment, receipts of a foreign currency in foreign countries between non-residents", we recommend amending the provision in this way.

Second, a "resident" in Article 3(1)14 should be reconceptualised. The current definition stating that "an individual who has a domicile or residence in Korea, and a legal entity whose main office is located in Korea" does not give any practical guidance when drawing contour lines of the element. Also, we observe that Article 10 of enforcement decree of the Act, which sets forth some specific rules to determine a resident depending on nationality and a residency period, often fails to give a clear definition on the concept. In fact, it is nearly impossible to present any clear and accurate criteria for judging the status of a person in consideration of every single possible case. Thus, it would be better to make it clear that "source of income" (or economic activity) is one of key elements to determine the residence, and define the particular sub-conditions to constitute the element under its enforcement decree. This is what both the Supreme Court and the governmental authority also recognised. Therefore, it is expected that amending the provision in such manner likely enhance the predictability of the law.

Third, the term "securities in foreign currency" in Article 3(1)8 has to extend its coverage scope to currency-linked foreign securities whose value is tied to Korean won. This is to clarify that the FETA also applies to any transactions that are performed in a foreign country but have an effect in Korea. In doing so, aforementioned issue of the "supremacy of law" and confusion surrounding the scope of "securities in foreign currency" will be resolved.

5.1.3 Repeal and Replace the *Pre-trades* Reporting with the *Post-trades* Reporting

Taking into account the fact that the government operates the "foreign exchange information concentration agency" that collects every data regarding cross-border payments or receipts on a real time basis, and because of the need to facilitate FX transactions by reducing regulatory burden, the existing pre-trades reporting obligations should be abolished or much more simplified. Instead, the FX authority may resort to the post-trades reporting.

However, admittedly, there could be some exceptions. Any transactions, payments or receipts without going through a foreign exchange agency (e.g., exporting or importing means of payment or securities) carry the risk of omitting transactional data and creating regulatory voids. Accordingly, the government needs to impose *ex ante* reporting duty as currently required on those who engage in such a transaction. Moreover, for a resident's large sum of foreign currency borrowing or a non-resident's large scale of Korean won borrowing, imposing the pre-trades reporting obligations would be justifiable from the perspective of ensuring market stability.[144] But even so, given the drastically increased size of the economy and volume of FX transactions, a minimum threshold of the reporting should be adjusted upwards. For example, in case of foreign currency borrowing by a resident, the current trigger of $30 million could be raised to $50 million or more.[145]

5.1.4 Strengthen Punishment for Market Abuse Behaviours

Trading misconducts in the FX market, encompassing collusion, price manipulation, and dissemination of rumours, should be strictly prohibited, because they distort the market mechanism, seriously harming market integrity and investor protection. For this reason, the Korean FX law (FETA) today bans

144 Due to its importance, those who conduct such a transaction may as well report it directly to MOEF, not a foreign exchange bank or the Bank of Korea.

145 The rule of $30 million has been in effect since January 2006. However, the average daily trading volume of spot exchange of foreign exchange banks more than doubled from $9.7 billion in 2005 to $19.6 billion in 2017.

such malpractices in the spot FX transactions and offenders (herein, foreign exchange agencies) are severely punished through the imprisonment with labour or fines, or both. Truly, it has a great significance in that the Korean government has filled the regulatory void in the spot FX market with a statute, not merely resorting to self-regulation by industry.[146] However, the level of punishment under the FETA is rather lower compared to that of the Financial Investment Services and Capital Markets Act (FISCMA) that stipulates similar provisions. In actuality, the FISCMA provides that "any persons (who commits a violation of rules related to market abuse behaviours such as currency rigging) shall be punished by imprisonment with labour for at least one year or by a fine equivalent to three to five times the profit accrued or loss avoided by a violation: *Provided* that no profit accrued or loss is avoided by the violation, or it is impracticable to calculate such profit or loss, or where the amount equivalent to five times the profit accrued or loss avoided by a violation is not exceeding 500 million won, the upper limit of the fine shall be 500 million won".[147] But a wrongdoer in the FX market is punished "by imprisonment with labour for not more than five years or by a fine not exceeding 500 million won: *Provided* that the triple value of the object related to the violation exceeds 500 million won, the fine shall not be more than the triple value of such object" under the FETA. Ergo, we propose that the relevant penalty provision of the FETA should be strengthened as follows (see Table 15).[148]

Similarly, administrative penalty surcharges for violation of Article 10(2) of the FETA should be also raised up to the level of that the FISCMA. Indeed, while the FX law currently imposes restriction or suspension of the business for three months, or penalty surcharges not exceeding 50% of unjust enrichment on the offenders, the FISCMA provides that "the Financial Services Commission may impose a penalty surcharge not exceeding 500 million won on a person who violates the law of market abuse prohibitions: *Provided* that the amount equivalent to 1.5 times the profit (including unrealised gain; hereafter the same shall apply in this Article) accrued from a trade related to such

146 As previously noted, a spot FX contract is not regarded as a financial investment instrument in every jurisdiction, including Korea. Therefore, the spot FX transaction has long been outside the regulatory perimeter, as opposed to a derivative contract whose transaction is commonly regulated by the securities law (in Korea, the FISCMA). Article 10(2) of the FETA, which was introduced in 2017, provided a cure.

147 Art. 443 of the FISCMA.

148 In this case, the level of punishment for other violation of the law, that is, a breach of safeguard measures, is also heightened, but it seems sufficiently reasonable and justifiable, since they are emergency actions that may be only triggered in a time of national crisis.

TABLE 15 A proposal for an amendment of the FETA

Current law	Proposals for revisions
Article 27 (Penalty Provisions) (1) Any of the following persons shall be punished by imprisonment with labour for not more than five years or by a fine not exceeding five hundred million won. Provided that the triple value of the object related to the violation exceeds five hundred million won, the fine shall not be more than the triple value of such object: 1. Any person who conducts transactions in non-compliance with the basic exchange rate, etc. in violation of Article 5(2). 2. Any person who pays or receives money, or make transactions in violation of measures prescribed in Article 6(1)1. 3. Any person who violates obligations of safekeeping, deposit or sale according to measures prescribed in Article 6(1)2. 4. Any person who violates the obligation to collect claims according to measures prescribed in Article 6(1)3. 5. Any person who conducts capital transactions without obtaining permission according to the measures prescribed in Article 6(2) or after obtaining permission by fraudulent or other unjust means, or who has violated an obligation of deposit. 6. Any person who conducts foreign exchange affairs in violation of Article 10(2).	**Article 27 (Penalty Provisions)** (1) *Any of the following persons shall be punished by imprisonment with labour for at least one year or by a fine equivalent to three to five times the profit accrued or loss avoided by a violation: Provided, That where no profit accrued or loss is avoided by the violation, or it is impracticable to calculate such profit or loss, or where the amount equivalent to five times the profit accrued or loss avoided by a violation is not exceeding 500 million won, the upper limit of the fine shall be 500 million won.* 1~6. same as the left

violation or the loss avoided by such violation exceeds 500 million won, it may impose a penalty surcharge not exceeding the amount equivalent to 1.5 times the amount of profit or avoided loss".[149] Ergo, we propose that Article 429–2 of the FISCMA should be applied, *mutatis mutandis*, to relevant provision of the FETA (Article 12–2) and its enforcement decree (Article 23).

5.2 *A Legal Definition of Foreign Exchange Products as the Financial Investment Instruments*

Every FX product (or contract) is exposed to risk of potential loss of the principal, because it fluctuates in value constantly with exchange rate variability. In other words, the FX related instruments have "investment attributes". A natural question that then arises would be, "FX products can be defined as the financial investment instruments that are governed under the FISCMA (the Korean securities regulation law)?"[150] We note here that the FETA defines "foreign exchange" as means of international payment (e.g., foreign currency), securities, derivatives and claims in foreign currency, and the FISCMA classifies financial investment instruments into securities and derivatives.[151]

It would be needless to say that securities and derivative denominated (or settled) in foreign currency can be defined as financial investment instruments. A foreign stock or bond is a kind of securities under the FISCMA, and a currency forward or swap contract is also a kind of derivatives under the same Act.

However, interpretation of means of international payment, *inter alia,* a purchase or sale of foreign currency in spot FX market is a little bit tricky. Spot FX market is defined as "a market on which currencies are bought and sold for

149 Art. 429–2 of the FISCMA.

150 Article 3(1) of the FISCMA defines a financial investment instrument as "a right acquired by an agreement to pay money or any other thing with property value at a specific point in the present or in the future, with intent to earn a profit or avoid a loss, where there is an (investment) risk that the total amount of such money, etc., paid or payable, to acquire that right (excluding sums specified by Presidential Decree, such as sales commissions) may exceed the total amount of money, etc. already recovered or recoverable from such right (including sums specified by Presidential Decree, such as termination fees)".

151 The FISCMA recognises the difference between the two instruments as follows: while "securities means financial investment instruments issued by a Korean national or a foreigner, for which an investors does not owe any obligation to make any additional payment on any ground, in addition to the money, etc. that the investor paid at the time he or she acquires such instruments (excluding obligation of payment that the investor assumes by exercising a right to effectuate the trading of an underlying asset)", derivatives means contractual rights that investors "may owe the obligation to make an additional payment" depending on a nature or terms of condition of contracts.

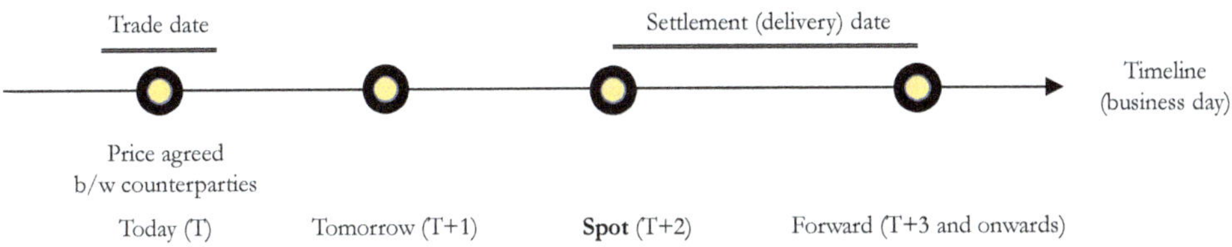

FIGURE 8 Timeline of foreign exchange spot transactions
SOURCE: KANG (2019) (FROM "RETHINKING SPOT FX REGULATION", PUBLISHED ON WWW.TANDFONLINE.COM. REPRODUCED AND REPUBLISHED WITH PERMISSION. ALL RIGHTS RESERVED)

quasi-immediate delivery (usually within two business days)".[152] On trade (or transactions) date, contractual terms, such as "transaction amounts, maturities, and invoice currencies are determined between counterparties", but the actual fund transfer does not occur until the settlement (or delivery) date (see Figure 8). Even if market exchange rate varies for this period of time, the contract price remains unchanged.[153] As a consequence, a party to the contract earns a profit and his or her counterparty make a loss, which implies that a spot FX transaction entails investment risk.

Evidence that spot FX contracts own investment attributes can be also found in actual patterns of spot trades of foreign exchange banks. According to the BIS survey results (see Figure 9), the total volume of spot FX transactions was averaged to be around $2.0 trillion on a daily basis, of which transactions between dealer banks and non financial customers were less than $0.2 trillion (8.0%). By contrast, spot transactions between dealer-banks recorded at $0.6 trillion (29.8%), and spot transactions between dealer banks and other financial institutions reached $1.2 trillion (62.2%). Noteworthy here is that a proportion that accounts for commercial demands by individuals or corporates is much lower than that explained by other speculative (or hedging) demands by foreign exchange banks. For instance, a larger part of spot FX transactions are driven by foreign exchange banks' squaring positions (i.e., hedging currency risk) in the interbank market after transactions with their clients in the customer market.

Having said that, there is a caveat: spot FX contracts are used not only for speculative (or hedging) needs but also for payment purposes, which complicates not only our understanding but also regulatory treatment of it. Rather, spot FX contracts are legally considered to be just "payment instruments" in

152 Kang, *supra* n. 8, p 234.
153 Ibid.

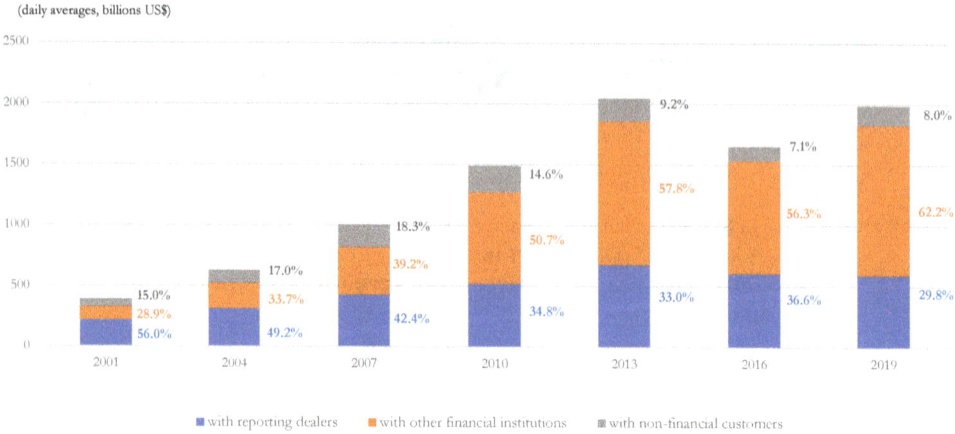

FIGURE 9 Spot FX transactions by counterparty
SOURCE: BIS (2019)

most jurisdictions. For example, the revised "European rules of markets in financial instruments directive (MiFID II) and regulation (MiFIR) suggest the following three criteria for FX contracts to be defined as a spot contract: (i) standard market practice/delivery period (for major currency pairs, T + 2 business days), (ii) security conversion transactions (in recognition of a longer settlement cycle than T + 2, but being subject to a cap of 5 days in order to avoid creating regulatory loopholes), and (iii) payment purpose".[154] In particular, the European rule makes it clear that "MiFID is intended to cover financial instruments, but not payment instruments, and international payments for trade and exports should not be unduly burdened".[155] This leads us to an argument that a spot FX contract should not be considered a financial instrument, as it is a means to facilitate international transactions, largely serving non-investment or commercial purpose.

The US authority's regulatory stance is not different. Spot FX contracts are outside the perimeter of the Commodity Exchange Act that regulates the trading of derivatives contracts.[156] Moreover, the regulatory authority (in this case, the CFTC) recognised a longer securities conversion period than the European standard.[157] Furthermore, the Treasury department gave authentic

154 Ibid.

155 See the Annex 9: A harmonised definition for FX spot contracts in EC (2016).

156 17 CFR § 1.3 (2012).

157 The CFTC issued a no action letter that indicates that the security and related foreign currency transactions with a settlement cycle of T + 7 business days might be considered as a *bona fide* spot foreign exchange transaction (CFTC Letter No. 13-13, No-Action (2 May 2013)).

TABLE 16 A proposal for an amendment of the FISCMA

Current law	Proposals for revisions
Article 3 (Financial Investment Instruments) (2) The financial investment instruments as defined in paragraph (1) are classified as follows: 1. Securities; 2. Derivatives (a) Exchange-traded derivatives (b) Over-the-counter derivatives 2-2. *<New item>*	**Article 3 (Financial Investment Instruments)** (2) The financial investment instruments as defined in paragraph (1) are classified as follows: 1. Securities (*including "securities in foreign currency" defined in the FETA*); 2. Derivatives (*including "derivatives in foreign currency" defined in the FETA*) (a) Exchange-traded derivatives (b) Over-the-counter derivatives 2-2. *The term "underlying assets" in this Act means any of the following*: (a) Financial investment instruments; (b) Currency (including any foreign currency); (c) Ordinary commodities (referring to agricultural products, livestock products, fisheries products, forestry products, mining products, energy, goods manufactured or processed with such products as raw materials, and other similar goods); (d) Credit risk (referring to a change in credit due to a change in the credit rating, bankruptcy, debt readjustment, etc. of a party or third party); (e) Other risk that is natural, environmental, or economic phenomena, which can be computed or assessed by price, interest, indicator, or unit in a reasonable and appropriate manner.

TABLE 16 A proposal for an amendment of the FISCMA (*cont.*)

Current law	Proposals for revisions
Article 4 (Securities) (10) The term "underlying assets" in this Act means any of the following: 1~5. ellipsis	**Article 4 (Securities)** (*10*) *<delete>*

interpretation that FX forwards (excluding non-deliverable forwards, NDF) and FX swap contracts in addition to spot FX should be considered as not falling within the scope of the CFTC regulations for the reason that they "generally trade in a highly liquid, efficient, and transparent inter-bank market that is characterised by a high degree of electronic trading".[158]

Taken together, it requires caution to legally define a spot FX contract as a financial instrument. Above all, it could be a dangerous idea for a country to regulate spot transactions alone to the same level with derivatives, since spot exchanges will be exempt from strong and rigorous enforcement of the strictest financial law in every other jurisdiction. Therefore, let us deal separately with a spot FX contract.[159] That is, we propose here that "securities and derivatives in foreign currency" should be expressly defined as financial investment instruments under the FISCMA (see Table 16).[160] In addition, as it is better to explain the term "derivatives" and "underlying assets" in tandem, the current provision of Article 4(10) needs to be moved below the subparagraph 2 of Article 3.

5.3 *An Incorporation of Procedural Regulations into Anti-money Laundering Legislation*

On the premise of replacing the *pre-trades* reporting system with the *post-trades* reporting system under the FETA, the area where functional adjustments need to be made accordingly is the anti-money laundering (AML) legislations.[161] Money laundering is generally defined as "the processing of the criminal proceeds to disguise their illegal origins", and foreign exchange instruments are

158 US Treasury Department, *supra* n. 39.

159 Nonetheless, market abuse behaviours in spot FX market will be regulated under Article 10(2) of the FETA.

160 This has a regulatory significance in that doing so clarifies the status of the national securities law, not an administrative rule of other law, as a governing law of every financial investment product and the related business.

161 AML legislation usually includes combating the financing of terrorism (CFT) policy measures, and it is often thus called AML/CFT control.

popular means for this illegitimate act.[162] Therefore, these two legal systems are closely related to each other.

On a related note, Article 2(5) of the Act on Reporting and Using Specified Financial Transaction Information (ARUSFTI) stipulates that money laundering means "disguising the fact of acquisition and disposal of assets or the cause thereof, or concealing such assets for the purpose of committing crimes, or evading taxes payable under the tax-related statutes". Illegal assets here are "criminal proceeds, etc. under subparagraph 4 of Article 2 of the Act on Regulation and Punishment of Criminal Proceeds Concealment (ARPCPC), or funds for terrorism under subparagraph 1 of Article 2 of the Act on Prohibition against the Financing of Terrorism and Proliferation of Weapons of Mass Destruction (APFTPWMD)": where criminal proceeds under the ARPCPC includes "funds or property concerning crime of property moving to a foreign country" under Article 4 of the Act on the Aggravated Punishment of Specific Economic Crimes (AAPSEC), and "funds or property related to raising, transporting, or keeping funds" for terrorism under Article 5–2 of the APFTPWMD.

Noteworthy here is that the provision of Article 4 of the AAPSEC is most likely to be examined concurrently with the FETA in the sense that it punishes a violator who "moves property, in violation of statutes, to a foreign country, or hoards any property that should be introduced into Korea by concealing or disposing of it in a foreign country". Also, the APFTPWMD must be considered together with the FETA. This is because it requires the government's permission for "a (designated) person subject to restrictions on financial transactions" to conduct a FX transaction.

In this respect, it seems reasonable that the FX authority incorporates procedural measures (such as reporting, confirmation, permission) of the FETA into the anti-money laundering legislations to regulate illicit overseas transfer.

5.3.1 Regulate Transactions Subject to Pre-trades Reporting/Confirmation under the ARUSFTI

Article 1 of the ARUSFTI stipulates that the purpose of this Act is to provide rules regarding "reports and use of specified financial transaction information necessary to regulate money laundering and financing of terrorism through financial transactions, thereby preventing crimes and firmly establishing a sound and transparent financial system". This implies that most procedural measures contained in the FETA (such as reporting, confirmation) could be taken under the ARUSFTI. That is, the government can effectively monitor and fight against illicit fund flows using foreign exchanges with the aid of

162 A detailed explanation of definition, methods, and effects on general societies of money laundering is available at https://www.fatf-gafi.org/faq/moneylaundering/.

monitoring and sanctions scheme prepared for the anti-money laundering law. Of course, it may be questioned whether such reasoning is valid in that the purpose of ARUSFTI and the FETA is not entirely identical but they shed lights on somewhat different side of the financial transactions: the reporting system under the former Act (ARUSFTI) aims at preventing money laundering based on the exchange of cash and financial assets and provide *ex post* relief, whereas the reporting system under the latter Act (FETA) aims at obtaining every possible transactional data of foreign exchanges for monitoring purposes, and when necessary, at taking timely and appropriate policy actions. However, it should be noted that the reality is that almost all information regarding cross-border capital flows is, as previously discussed, collected by the BOK in quasi real-time, and today, the FX law violations concerning a failure of reporting to the relevant authority are frequently involved with money laundering cases. In light of this, we can safely say that mandating reports in connection with foreign exchange transactions overlaps in good part between the two legal systems. Indeed, as the Supreme Court once held, an implicit reason why the FETA stipulates a host of procedural regulations is to deter illegitimate funds transfer (such as flight of domestic property, tax evasion).[163]

The ARUSFTI already puts some measures in ready to monitor as well as crack down on illegal transfers of foreign exchange, imposing regulatory obligations on financial institutions; that is, reporting on transactions of suspected illegal assets (Article 4), measures by financial companies (Article 5), and customer due diligence for financial companies (Article 5-2). First, Article 4(1) of the ARUSFTI stipulates that "in a case that there exist any reasonable grounds to suspect that an asset which has been received in relation to any financial transaction (including foreign exchange) is illegal, or there are any reasonable grounds to suspect that the other party to a financial transaction, etc. engages in money laundering or financing of terrorism, financial institutions must report such fact to the commissioner of the FIU without delay".[164] In this case, financial institutions and employees that have filed a report are exempt from liability for damages to the counterparty to the financial transactions at issue, unless "a false report has been filed by intent or gross negligence".[165]

---

163 The highest court ruled that "the likelihood that the FX transaction in question is involved with illicit overseas transfer must be also considered, since the reason why the FETA stipulates the obligation to report before engaging in transactions is to prevent illegal transfers of foreign exchange". See the Supreme Court Decision 2013Do9374 delivered on 28 August 2014.

164 Article 3(1)3 of enforcement decree of the ARUSFTI provides that the term "financial transactions" in this Act includes FX transactions.

165 Art. 4(7) of the ARUSFTI.

Second, Article 5 of the ARUSFTI requires financial institutions to implement various measures to reinforce internal control system for the purpose of facilitating the "suspicious transaction report (STR)" in accordance with Article 4 of the Act and effectively preventing money laundering and financing of terrorism. The measures that the Act enumerates include "establishing an internal reporting system, designating a person-in-charge, implementing procedures and business conduct guidelines, and educating or training the executive officers and employees".

Third, Article 5-2 of the ARUSFTI mandates that financial institutions exercise reasonable care when dealing with their customer transactions, requiring them to verify the client's personal information including information about a natural person finally governing and controlling the client (or the "actual owner"): this rule is also known as the customer due diligence (CDD). Additionally, financial institutions should verify the purpose and the source for transactions when "it is likely for a customer to commit money laundering or financing of terrorism, including where it is doubt that the customer is the actual owner": this rule is also known as the enhanced due diligence (EDD). It should be noted here that the correspondent banking of foreign exchange is recognised by the government as a financial transaction entailing a high risk of money laundering and financing or terrorism. This is because a FX transaction usually takes the form of international payments or receipts between banks whose countries have varying degrees of AML/CFT rules and conventions. Therefore, transactional data collected by the FEIS (controlled by the BOK) and the related information from any source must be checked closely and verified.

Taken together, it is seemingly inevitable that the role of the ARUSFTI is increasingly stressed and its regulatory scope is more and more expanded in fighting against illegitimate FX transactions. In particular, unconventional or anomalous FX transactions that irregularly occur (e.g., setoffs, the third-party payments or receipts) should be monitored closely enough not to create any significant regulatory voids. As a matter of course, financial institutions should perform the EDD to these transactions, and those who fail to take such reasonable care for AML/CFT risk mitigation need to be more severely penalised than those who are in breach of CDD.[166] Ergo, we propose that the provision of financial institutions' duties regarding verification of the identity of customers should be amended as follows (see Table 17).

166 With regard to this, a person who fails to take verification measures in violation of EDD is currently subject to an "administrative fine not exceeding 100 million won", whereas a person who fails to take verification measures in violation of CDD is subject to an "administrative fine not exceeding 30 million won" (Art. 20 of the ARUSFTI).

TABLE 17 A proposal for an amendment of the ARUSFTI

Current law	Proposals for revisions
Article 5-2 (Customer Due Diligence for Financial Companies) (1) As part of due diligence to guard against the risk of money laundering and financing of terrorism using financial transactions, etc. each financial company, etc. shall take the measures classified as follows. In such cases, any financial company, etc. shall prepare and implement work guidelines for such measures: 1. Where a customer opens an account or makes a one-time financial transaction, etc. in at least an amount prescribed by Presidential Decree: The following matters shall be verified: (a) Customer's personal information and others related thereto which are prescribed by Presidential Decree; (b) A natural person finally governing and controlling a customer (hereafter in this Article referred to as an "actual owner") and others related thereto: Provided, That, where a customer is a legal person or organisation, matters prescribed by Presidential Decree; 2. Where it is likely for a customer to commit money laundering or financing of terrorism, including where it is doubt that the customer is the actual owner: (a) The items of subparagraph 1; (b) Matters determined and publicly notified by the Commissioner of the Korea Financial Intelligence Unit including the purpose of a financial transaction, etc. and the source of funds for transactions (limited to the scope deemedreasonable by a financial	**Article 5-2 (Customer Due Diligence for Financial Companies)** (1) As part of due diligence to guard against the risk of money laundering and financing of terrorism using financial transactions, etc. each financial company, etc. shall take the measures classified as follows. In such cases, any financial company, etc. shall prepare and implement work guidelines for such measures: 1. Where a customer opens an account or makes a one-time financial transaction, etc. in at least an amount prescribed by Presidential Decree: The following matters shall be verified: (a) Customer's personal information and others related thereto which are prescribed by Presidential Decree; (b) A natural person finally governing and controlling a customer (hereafter in this Article referred to as an "actual owner") and others related thereto: Provided, That, where a customer is a legal person or organisation, matters prescribed by Presidential Decree; 2. Where it is likely for a customer to commit money laundering or financing of terrorism, including where it is doubt that the customer is the actual owner, *or he or she employs "unconventional method of transactions"*: (a)~(b) same as the left

TABLE 17 A proposal for an amendment of the ARUSFTI (*cont.*)

Current law	Proposals for revisions
company etc., having regard to the risks of money laundering and financing of terrorism;	
3. As is	3. same as the left

TABLE 18 A proposal for an amendment of enforcement Decree of the ARUSFTI

Current law	Proposals for revisions
Article 10-2 (Cases Requiring Verification of Identity of Customers) (1)~(2) As is (3) *<New item>* [Move the existing (3) to (4)]	**Article 10-2 (Cases Requiring Verification of Identity of Customers)** (1)~(2) same as the left (3) *The term "unconventional method of transactions" under Article 5-2(1) of the Act means transactions, payments or receipts that are considered to deviate from the customer's usual pattern of activities or commonly observed market practices, including set-offs, the third-party payments or receipts, and those transactions without going through a foreign exchange agency.*

Also, we propose that Article 10-2 of enforcement decree, which stipulates matters delegated by Article 5-2 of the ARUSFTI, should be amended accordingly as follows (see Table 18).

5.3.2 Regulate Transactions Subject to Permission under the APFTPWMD

Article 15(2) of the FETA and its enforcement decree stipulate that the finance minister "may require residents and non-residents who intend to make payment from Korea to a foreign country, or residents who intend to make payment to non-residents or to receive payment from non-residents, to obtain permission of the governor of the Bank of Korea, where it is inevitable for the faithful fulfilment of treaties concluded by Korea, and of generally recognised international laws and regulations, or where it is necessary for especially contributing to international endeavour for the maintenance of international peace and security".[167] However, it should be noted that a very similar provision can also be found in Article 4 of the APFTPWMD, which requires anyone to obtain a permit from the Financial Service Commission (or the governor of the Bank of Korea) to engage in financial transactions with a "person subject to restrictions on financial transactions" who mainly commits terrorism-related offences that jeopardise international peace and public safety. Even though the latter addresses this matter on a narrower focus on terrorism financing, it can be said that the two legal provisions are in effect meant to regulate the similar targets, largely sharing objects of application in common.

Therefore, if legislators interpret that "persons subject to restrictions on financial transactions" that the Financial Service Commission designates include "special designated nationals" that the finance minister labels in accordance with the administrative rules of "A Guideline for Payment and Receipt Permission for Promotion of International Peace and Security", and engrave as such, which we argue they can, the APFTPWMD would be able to integrate the permission rule of the FETA.[168] Ergo, we propose that Article 4 of the APFTPWMD should be amended as follows (see Table 19).

5.3.3 Amend the Rule of the ARUSFTI in furtherance of Authority of the FIU

In order to crack down on illegal funds transfer and to promote the authority's monitoring capacity, the accessibility of related governmental organisations to the information collected by the FEIS (under the BOK) should be enhanced. In particular, the role of the Financial Intelligence Unit (FIU), whose mission is to extract transactions suspected of violation of laws, will be of great importance. However, unfortunately, the scope of information or data available to this agency is rather limited under current legislation, being an obstacle to effective monitoring activities for deterrent and preventive control of illicit overseas transfer.[169]

For example, although Article 9(1) of the ARUSFTI stipulates that the head of the foreign exchange information concentration agency (or the governor of the Bank of Korea) and the commissioner of the Customs Service should

167 See also Art. 23(1) of the FETA and Art. 37(3)7 of enforcement decree of the Act.

168 The Ministry of Economy and Finance prepares this guideline in order to sanction those who are designated by the finance minister, following what the UN Security Council, US president (Executive Order), or the EU Council determines.

169 The Korean government acknowledges the need to improve the current law for this reason. According to the authority, "as each governmental organisation accesses to analyse the information collected by the FEIS, problems arise that duplicative data management or omission of material information hinders the agency from detecting illegal transactions in time". See MOEF, *supra* n. 63.

TABLE 19 A proposal for an amendment of the APFTPWMD

Current law	Proposals for revisions
Article 4 (Designation, etc. of Persons Subject to Restrictions on Financial Transactions, etc.) (1) Where the Financial Services Commission deems that an individual, corporation or organisation is related to any act falling under any of the items of subparagraph 1 of Article 2 or the proliferation of weapons of mass destruction (hereinafter referred to as "proliferation of weapons of mass destruction, etc.") and that such individual, corporation or organisation falls under any of the following, it may designate the individual, corporation or organisation as a person whose acts referred to in paragraph (4) 1 and 2 are restricted (hereinafter referred to as "person subject to restrictions on financial transactions, etc."), and publicly announce such designation: 1. Where restriction on the proliferation of weapons of mass destruction, etc. is necessary to comply with treaties to which Korea is a party, or generally accepted international laws in good faith; 2. Where restriction on the proliferation of weapons of mass destruction, etc. is necessary to especially contribute to international efforts to sustain international peace and security.	**Article 4 (Designation, etc. of Persons Subject to Restrictions on Financial Transactions, etc.)** (1) Where the Financial Services Commission deems that *a resident or a non-resident is related to any act falling under any of the following*, it may designate the individual, corporation or organisation as a person whose acts referred to in paragraph (4) 1 and 2 are restricted (hereinafter referred to as "person subject to restrictions on financial transactions, etc."), and publicly announce such designation: 1. *Where it is inevitable for the faithful fulfilment of treaties concluded by Korea, and of generally recognised international laws and regulations;* 2. *Where it is necessary for especially contributing to international endeavour for the maintenance of international peace and security.*
(2)~(5) As is	(2)~(5) same as the left
(6) When any person designated and publicly announced as a person subject to restrictions on financial transactions,	(6) *When it is no longer necessary to regulate any person designated and publicly announced as a person subject to*

TABLE 19 A proposal for an amendment of the APFTPWMD (*cont.*)

Current law	Proposals for revisions
etc. pursuant to paragraph (1) is no longer related to the proliferation of weapons of mass destruction, etc., the Financial Services Commission shall revoke such designation, and publicly announce it. In such cases, the main sentence of paragraph	*restrictions on financial transactions, etc. pursuant to paragraph (1)*, the Financial Services Commission shall revoke such designation, and publicly announce it. In such cases, the main sentence of paragraph
(2) shall apply *mutatis mutandis* to the revocation of designation as a person subject to restrictions on financial transactions, etc.	(2) shall apply *mutatis mutandis* to the revocation of designation as a person subject to restrictions on financial transactions, etc.

"notify the Commissioner of the Korea Financial Intelligence Unit of the data related to the reports and notifications under the FETA", the scope of the data subject to notification and the procedures of notification are determined by the head of foreign exchange information concentration agency after consultation with the finance minister.[170] Furthermore, requests for provision of data for the analysis of suspicious FX transactions are merely possible to the head of the relevant financial institutions to the minimum extent necessary, not directly to the head of the foreign exchange information concentration agency.[171]

Admittedly, there must be some backstop, but it should also not be a hindrance to exercising appropriate authority. The commissioner of the FIU needs to be given a wider access to data provided by the foreign exchange information concentration agency, and if necessary, it should be able to request not only to the financial institutions but also directly to the agency (i.e., the BOK). The concerns about any potential infringement of privacy or abusive power of the FIU could be more effectively resolved by operating a well-designed "intelligence analysis council" and the enhanced oversight of the National Assembly.[172]

170 Art. 9(1) of the ARUSFTI and Art. 11(2)2 of its enforcement decree.

171 Art. 13(3) of the ARUSFTI.

172 An intelligence analysis council under the control of the commissioner of the FIU is established to deliberate on the provision of specified financial transaction information

Ergo, we propose that Article 13 of the ARUSFTI should be amended as follows (see Table 20).

TABLE 20 A proposal for an amendment of the ARUSFTI

Current law	Proposals for revisions
Article 13 (Requests for Provision of Data) (3) In analysing specified financial transaction information, the Commissioner of the Korea Financial Intelligence Unit may request the head of a financial company, etc., to provide the information or data on financial transaction, etc. involving transactions arising from foreign exchange affairs prescribed in the Foreign Exchange Transactions Act in writing stating the following, only where matters reported or provided are deemed to satisfy the requirements set forth in Article 4(1): 1. The trader's personal details; 2. Purpose of the use of information; 3. Details of information or data related to financial transactions requested.	**Article 13 (Requests for Provision of Data)** (3) In analysing specified financial transaction information, the Commissioner of the Korea Financial Intelligence Unit may request the head of a financial company, etc. *and the head of the foreign exchange information concentration agency* to provide the information or data on financial transaction, etc. involving transactions arising from foreign exchange affairs prescribed in the Foreign Exchange Transactions Act in writing stating the following, only where matters reported or provided are deemed to satisfy the requirements set forth in Article 4(1): 1~3. same as the left

to the Prosecutor General, etc. The council is comprised of three public officials of the Korea Financial Intelligence Unit: a Commissioner of the FIU, a general manager in charge of the review and analysis, and a person recommended by the Chief Justice of the Supreme Court among judges with at least 10 years of experiences and appointed by the Commissioner of the FIU.

In addition, we propose that Article 11 of enforcement decree, which stipulates matters delegated by Article 13 of the ARUSFTI, should be amended accordingly as follows (see Table 21).

TABLE 21 A proposal for an amendment of enforcement decree of the ARUSFTI

Current law	Proposals for revisions
Article 11 (Notification of Records, etc. of Foreign Exchange Transactions)	**Article 11 (Notification of Records, etc. of Foreign Exchange Transactions)**
(2) The scope of records subject to notification pursuant to Article 9(2) of the Act shall be as follows: 1. Records which are permitted by the Governor of the Bank of Korea or reported to the heads of customs offices with respect to the exportation or importation of the means of payment, etc. under Article 17 of the Foreign Exchange Transactions Act;	(2) The scope of records subject to notification pursuant to Article 9(2) of the Act *refers to the records which are permitted by the Governor of the Bank of Korea or reported to the heads of customs offices with respect to the exportation or importation of the means of payment, etc. under Article 17 of the Foreign Exchange Transactions Act.*
2. Records which are necessary for the Korea Financial Intelligence Unit to perform its services and determined by the head of foreign exchange information concentration agency after consultation with the Minister of Strategy and Finance, from among those concentrated to the head of foreign exchange information concentration agency under Article 21 of the Foreign Exchange Transactions Act.	2. *<delete>*
(3) The Governor of the Bank of Korea, the heads of customs offices and the head of foreign exchange information concentration agency shall notify, in an electronic document, the Commissioner of the Korea Financial Intelligence Unit of the records referred to in paragraph (2) every	(3) The Governor of the Bank of Korea, the heads of customs offices and the head of foreign exchange information concentration agency shall notify, in an electronic document, the Commissioner of the Korea Financial Intelligence Unit of the records referred to *the Article 9(1) of the Act* every month not later than

TABLE 21 A proposal for an amendment of enforcement decree of the ARUSFTI (*cont.*)

Current law	Proposals for revisions
month not later than the tenth day of the following month: Provided, That where the Commissioner of the Korea Financial Intelligence Unit determines separately the time, methods, etc. of such notification after consultation with the Governor of the Bank of Korea, the heads of customs offices and the head of foreign exchange information concentration agency, respectively, it shall prevail.	the tenth day of the following month: Provided, That where the Commissioner of the Korea Financial Intelligence Unit determines separately the time, methods, etc. of such notification after consultation with the Governor of the Bank of Korea, the heads of customs offices and the head of foreign exchange information concentration agency, respectively, it shall prevail.

6 Conclusion

The overarching objectives of foreign exchange market regulations are (i) to maintain equilibrium in the balance of payments while stabilising the value of currency, and (ii) to fight against market abuse and conduct risk in the most lightly regulated trading venue. The former refers to the policy objective that FX authorities have traditionally sought to achieve, which is especially crucial for small open economies that would most likely suffer from *original sin* of lack of anchor currency when faced with external disturbances. This is why the Korean government has historically-long operated FX law in favour of capital controls, and, more recently, macroprudential policies with a special focus on managing short-term external debt. The latter aims at promoting market integrity and consumer protection by deterring and preventing currency market manipulation. Foreign exchange rates are not kept stable but are constantly moving. Given that a small group of the largest dealer banks may have great influence on supply and demand in the spot foreign exchange markets, a heavy reliance on self-regulation is insufficient as the 2013 global FX rigging scandal has revealed. This is why the Korean government recently introduced a new provision of the market abuse prohibitions into the FETA.

The Korean government has made a great effort to eliminate many existing control measures and facilitate cross border trades, expecting the reform to enhance the market depth and in turn to contribute to fortifying resilience of the FX market in times of crisis. Indeed, it is commonly accepted that the

Korean FX market regulation is, at least *de jure*, placed on a par with that of most advanced economies. However, despite significant progress made to date, there are still many remaining unresolved problems and the rapidly changing financial environment poses new challenges for legal institutions, which calls for further reform. First, the Korean FX law (the FETA) should be overhauled in a way that it commits to serving paramount goals of FX regulation referred above, and it also has to delegate other ancillary functions, such as curbing illegal funds transfer, to more properly designed financial laws. More specifically, the Act needs to transpose most provisions related to monitoring international payments and receipts into anti-money laundering legislations that mainly target suspicious financial activities. Furthermore, enormously complex procedural regulations, particularly as to *pre-trades* report (or notification) obligations, should be repealed and replaced with *post-trades* report with only minor exceptions. Given that the government operates a highly centralised information gathering system that enables authorities to timely monitor and analyse every cross-border transactional data, the usefulness of *ex ante* reporting is largely limited, and the demerits of imposing heavy compliance and reporting burden on financial consumers has proven to outweigh the informational benefits. Another reason why this reform has particular significance is that eliminating the pre-trades reporting obligations can resolve a critical issue of *supremacy of law* in that the procedural regulations are entirely made by the government executive, not legislators. Taking into account the fact that delegated administrative rules are prone to lack of democratic legitimacy, and particularly a deviation from the stated procedure can be prosecuted in criminal court, the administrator-made law can generate a serious problem in terms of *nulla poena sine lege* (no penalty without law) principle.

Second, in recognition of their investment attributes, every FX product (or contract) other than spot exchange should be expressly defined as a "financial investment instrument" in the FISCMA. In doing so, all derivative contracts denominated in foreign currencies (such as FX forward, options and swaps) will be covered in the Act and market participants would be more broadly and effectively protected by well-established market abuse regulations.

Third, as the "foreign exchange banks" that constitute the backbone of the Korean FX regulatory system are destined to lose their privileged monopoly power in the currency market and give some way to non-bank financial institutions or non-financial entities (e.g., fintech companies), competition for business in the market is getting more and more fierce. With regard to this, it would be crucial to level a playing field among industry participants without prejudice to the objective of market stability. This is the most challenging task the Korean government today faces up to, and it is expected that overall business environment will change considerably depending on how to define the scope and delimitation of foreign exchange business that each player is permitted to operate.

Taken together, foreign exchange transactions cannot be properly regulated by a single law but rather its policy objectives can be fully achieved only when other financial laws work congruently with foreign exchange law and regulations. Korean lawmakers and government should reassess the current status of the FX regulatory landscape and overhaul the whole legal system. Such a holistic approach would enable the government to effectively manage FX risk stemming from a myriad of disruptions in fast-evolving financial environments through building robust market and regulatory system.

Bibliography

Albanese C (2015) Forex Scandal Drives Shift to Algo Trading. *Wall Street Journal* (28 September 2015) https://www.wsj.com/articles/forex-scandal-drives-shift-to-algo-trading-1443444666.

Bank for International Settlement (BIS) (2019) Triennial Central Bank Survey: Foreign exchange turnover in April 2019 (16 Sep 2019).

Bank of Korea (BOK) (2013) Press release: Implementing the New Foreign Exchange Information System (July 2013).

Bank of Korea (BOK) (2016) Foreign Exchange System and Market in Korea (January 2016).

Bank of Korea (BOK) (2018) Understanding the Korean foreign exchange system. the BOK Friday Lecture series No. 767 (16 November 2018).

Bank of Korea (BOK) (2022) Press release: Foreign Exchange Banks' trades in 2021, the Bank of Korea (Jan. 26, 2022).

Chrispin S (2015) Forex Scandal: How to Rig the Market. *BBC* (20 May 2015) https://www.bbc.com/news/business-26526905.

European Commission (EC) (2016) Commission Staff Working Document Impact Assessment Accompanying Delegated Regulation, Supplementing Regulation (EU) No 600/2014 (18 May 2016) https://ec.europa.eu/smart-regulation/impact/ia_carried_out/docs/ia_2016/swd_2016_0157_en.pdf.

European Securities and Markets Authority (ESMA) (2015) Final Report: Draft Regulatory and Implementing Technical Standards MiFID II/MiFIR (28 September 2015) https://www.esma.europa.eu/sites/default/files/library/2015/11/2015-esma-1464_-_final_report_-_draft_rts_and_its_on_mifid_ii_and_mifir.pdf.

European Securities and Markets Authority (ESMA) (2020) ESMA Publishes Outcome of MAR Review (24 September 2020) https://www.esma.europa.eu/press-news/esma-news/esma-publishes-outcomes-mar-review.

Financial Conduct Authority (FCA) (2016) Speech by Edwin Schooling Latter, Head of Markets Policy at the FCA, delivered at FX Week Europe. (30 November 2016) https://www.fca.org.uk/news/speeches/conduct-risk-fx-markets.

Financial Stability Board (FSB) (2014) Final Report on Foreign Exchange Benchmarks (30 September 2014) https://www.fsb.org/2014/09/r140930/.

Financial Supervisory Service (FSS) (2019) Press release: Violation cases of the foreign exchange transaction regulations in 2018 (5 March 2019).

Global Foreign Exchange Committee (GFXC) (2017) FX Global Code (May 2017) https://www.globalfxc.org/docs/fx_global_may17.pdf.

Goodhart C, Hartman P, Llewellyn D, Suarez LR, Weisbrod S (1998) Financial Regulation: Why, How and Where Now? Routledge.

HM Treasury, Bank of England, Financial Conduct Authority (2015) Fair and Effective Markets Review – Final Report (June 2015) https://www.bankofengland.co.uk/-/media/boe/files/report/2015/fair-and-effective-markets-review-final-report.pdf?la=en&hash=1985B00AA2221D81606668501E01EB0B0412403A.

HM Treasury, Bank of England, Financial Conduct Authority (2016) Fair and Effective Markets Review – Implementation Report (July 2016) https://www.bankofengland.co.uk/-/media/boe/files/report/2016/fair-and-effective-markets-review-implementation-report.pdf.

International Monetary Fund (IMF) (2004) Classification of Exchange Rate Arrangements and Monetary Policy Frameworks (June 30, 2004), https://www.imf.org/external/np/mfd/er/2004/eng/0604.htm.

International Monetary Fund (IMF) (2012) The Liberalisation and Management of Capital Flows: An Institutional View. *IMF Policy Papers* (14 November 2012) https://www.imf.org/external/np/pp/eng/2012/111412.pdf.

International Monetary Fund (IMF) (2017) Increasing Resilience to Large and Volatile Capital Flows: The Role of Macroprudential Policies. *IMF Policy Papers* (5 July 2017) https://www.imf.org/en/Publications/Policy-Papers/Issues/2017/07/05/pp060217-increasing-resilience-to-large-and-volatile-capital-flows.

International Monetary Fund (IMF) (2021) Annual Report on Exchange Arrangements and Exchange Restrictions 2020 (25 Aug 2021).

Jeanne O, Korinek A (2010) Managing Credit Booms and Busts: A Pigouvian Taxation Approach. *NBER Working Papers* No. 16377.

Kang M (2016) A Review of Prudential Regulation of Foreign Exchange in Korea. *The Korean Journal of Securities Law* 17(2): 547–573.

Kang M (2017) A Critical Review of Foreign Exchange Bank's Confirmation Obligation in Performing Duties. The Bank of Korea Legal Office.

Kang M (2019) Rethinking spot FX regulation. *Law and Financial Markets Review* 13(4): 234–243.

Kim L (2015) A Study on Collection-and-Recovery Order under the Foreign Exchange Transactions Act – Focusing on Legality of Theory of Comprehensive Collection-and-Recovery Order. *Kookmin Law Review* 28(2): 247–282.

Kim N (2010) Die Rechtstheorie der verwaltungsrechtlicher Anzeige – Problematik der Theorien und Rechtsprechungen -. *Gachon Law Review* 3(3): 113–137.

Kirtzman M (1999) Toward Defining an Asset Class. *Journal of Alternative Investments* 2: 79–82.

Korinek A (2018) Regulating Capital Flows to Emerging Markets: An Externality View. *Journal of International Economics* 111: 61–80.

Krugman PR (1979) A Model of Balance of Payments Crises. *Journal of Money, Credit and Banking* 11(3): 311–325.

Krugman PR, Obstfeld M, Melitz M (2014) International Economics: Theory and Policy. 10th edn, Pearson.

Lastra RM (2006) Legal Foundations of International Monetary Stability. Oxford University Press.

Lee MW (2007) Analysis of Scrutiny Standards for Constitutionality of Legislative Delegation and Such Cases Declared Unconstitutional. *The Justice* 96: 65–87.

Lowi TJ (1987) Two Roads to Serfdom: Liberalism, Conservatism, and Administrative Power. *American University Law Review* 36(2): 295–322.

Magud NE, Reinhart CM, Rogoff K (2011) Myth and Reality – A portfolio Balance Approach. *NBER Working Paper* No. 16805.

McGeever J (2017) TIMELINE-The global FX rigging scandal. *Reuters* (11 January 2017) https://www.reuters.com/article/global-currencies-scandal-idUSL5N1F14VV.

Milesi-Ferretti, G M. and Razin, A (1998) Current Account Reversals and Currency Crisis: Empirical Regularities. *IMF Working Paper* 98/1306620.

Ministry of Economy and Finance (MOEF) (2010) Press release: New macro-prudential measures to mitigate volatility of capital flows (14 June 2010).

Ministry of Economy and Finance (MOEF) (2015) Press release: FX transactions regulation reform to promote external transactions and support the competitiveness of financial industry (29 June 2015).

Ministry of Economy and Finance (MOEF) (2016a) Press release: Revisions to enforcement decree of the FETA and the FETR (15 March 2016).

Ministry of Economy and Finance (MOEF) (2016b) Press release: Revisions to FX Regulation Focus on Flexibility (16 June 2016).

Ministry of Economy and Finance (MOEF) (2017) Press release: Deputy Prime Minister and Minister of Economy and Finance of the ROK Talked with US Secretary of the Treasury (18 March 2017).

Ministry of Economy and Finance (MOEF) (2018) Press release: Reforming FX regulatory system (27 September 2018).

Ministry of Economy and Finance (MOEF) (2022) Press release: The Specified Enactment Direction of the New Foreign Exchange Act (5 July 2022).

Mundell RA (1963) Capital Mobility and Stabilisation Policy under Fixed and Flexible Exchange Rates. *Canadian Journal of Economics and Political Science* 29(4): 475–485.

Obstfeld M, Rogoff K (1996) Foundations of International Macroeconomics. MIT Press.

Potter SM (2015) Remarks at the 2015 FX Week Conference, New York City: Trends in Foreign Exchange Markets and the Challenges Ahead (14 July 2015) https://www.newyorkfed.org/newsevents/speeches /2015/pot150714.

Powers C (2016) Filling the Regulatory Void in the FX Spot Market: How Traders Rigged the Biggest Market in the World. *Fordham Urban Law Journal* 43: 139–193.

Proctor C (2005) Mann on the Legal Aspect of Money. 6th edn, Oxford University Press.

Quintana PG (2013) The Economics of Small Open Economies. Federal Reserve Bank of Philadelphia *Business Review* 96(4): 9–18.

Rey H (2015) Dilemma not Trilemma: The Global Financial Cycle and Monetary Policy Independence. *NBER Working Paper* No. 21162.

Schwarcz SL (2014) The Functional Regulation of Finance (Harvard Law School Forum on Corporate Governance, 16 June 2014) https://corpgov.law.harvard.edu/2011/06/09/supreme-court-holds-loss-causation-not-a-prerequisite-to-class-certification-in-fraud-cases/.

Seo MS (2018) The Origin of the Korean Foreign Exchange Control Law. *The Korean Journal of Financial Law* 15(3): 209–255.

Shubik M (1971) Pecuniary Externalities: A Game Theoretic Analysis. *American Economic Review* 61(4): 713–718.

Stout LA (2011) Derivatives and the Legal Origin of the 2008 Global Credit Crisis. *Harvard Business Law Review* 1: 1–38.

Tormey TA (1997) A Derivatives Dilemma: The Treasury Amendment Controversy and the Regulatory Status of Foreign Currency Options. *Fordham Law Review* 65: 2313–2379.

US Treasury Department (2012) Fact Sheet: Final Determination on Foreign Exchange Swaps and Forwards (16 November 2012) https://www.treasury.gov/press-center/press-releases/pages/tg1773.aspx.

Vaughan L, Finch G, Choudhury A (2013) Traders Said to Rig Currency Rates to Profit Off Clients. Bloomberg (12 June 2013) https://www.bloomberg.com/news/articles/2013-06-11/traders-said-to-rig-currency-rates-to-profit-off-clients.

www.ingramcontent.com/pod-product-compliance
Lightning Source LLC
Chambersburg PA
CBHW071355230926
51846CB00002B/571
9789004540293